# CODING GAMES

## in SCRATCH™

Content previously published in *Coding Games In Scratch* (2015)

## DK UK

**Senior editor** Ben Morgan
**Project art editor** Laura Brim
**Editors** Lizzie Davey, Ashwin Khurana, Steve Setford
**US editors** Jill Hamilton, Margaret Parrish
**Designers** Mabel Chan, Peter Radcliffe, Steve Woosnam-Savage
**Jacket design development manager** Sophia MTT
**Jacket editor** Claire Gell
**Producer, pre-production** Francesca Wardell
**Producer** Mary Slater
**Managing editor** Paula Regan
**Managing art editor** Owen Peyton Jones
**Publisher** Andrew Macintyre
**Associate publishing director** Liz Wheeler
**Art director** Karen Self
**Design director** Stuart Jackman
**Publishing director** Jonathan Metcalf

**Special Sales and Custom Publishing Manager** Michelle Baxter

## DK DELHI

**Project editor** Suefa Lee
**Project art editor** Parul Gambhir
**Editor** Sonia Yooshing
**Art editors** Sanjay Chauhan, Upasana Sharma
**Assistant art editor** Simar Dhamija
**Senior DTP designers** Harish Aggarwal, Vishal Bhatia
**Senior managing editor** Rohan Sinha
**Managing art editor** Sudakshina Basu
**Pre-production manager** Balwant Singh
**Jacket designer** Dhirendra Singh
**Managing jackets editor** Saloni Singh

Content previously published in *Coding Games In Scratch* (2015)
This edition published in the United States in 2016 by
DK Publishing, 345 Hudson Street,
New York, New York 10014

Copyright © 2016 Dorling Kindersley Limited
A Penguin Random House Company

002—295913—Jan/2016

Published in Great Britain by Dorling Kindersley Limited.

A catalog record for this book is available from the Library of Congress.

ISBN: 978-1-4654-5451-5

DK books are available at special discounts when purchased in bulk for sales
promotions, premiums, fund-raising, or educational use. For details, contact: DK
Publishing Special Markets, 345 Hudson Street, New York, New York 10014
or SpecialSales@dk.com

Printed in China

A WORLD OF IDEAS:
**SEE ALL THERE IS TO KNOW**

www.dk.com

# ABOUT THE AUTHOR:

**DR. JON WOODCOCK MA (OXON)** has a degree in physics
from the University of Oxford and a PhD in computational
astrophysics from the University of London. He started
coding at the age of eight and has programmed all kinds
of computers, from single-chip microcontrollers to
world-class supercomputers. His many projects include
giant space simulations, research in high-tech companies,
and intelligent robots made from junk. Jon has a passion
for science and technology education, giving talks on
space and running computer programming clubs in
schools. He has worked on numerous science and
technology books as a contributor and consultant,
including DK's *Computer Coding for Kids* and *Computer
Coding Made Easy*.

# Contents

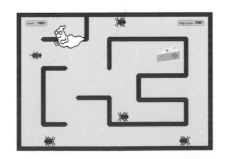

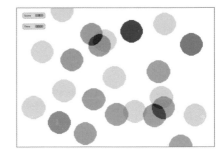

Find out more at:
**www.dk.com/computercoding**

# Getting
# started

# What makes a good game?

Some games have a magical quality that makes you want to play them time and again. Game designers call it playability. To make a game with great playability, you need to think about all the ingredients that make up the game and how they work together.

I have the perfect recipe!

◁ **Characters**

In most games, the player uses an on-screen character to enter the game world. It could an animal, a princess, a racecar, or even just a simple bubble. To create a sense of danger or competition, such games usually also have enemy characters that the player has to defeat or escape from.

△ **Mechanics**

These are the "verbs" in a game—actions such as running, jumping, flying, capturing objects, casting spells, and using weapons. The mechanics are the core of the game, and well-designed mechanics make a good game.

△ **Objects**

Nearly all games include objects, from stars and coins that boost health or scores to keys that unlock doors. Not all objects are good—some get in the player's way, sap their health, or steal their treasures. Objects can also work together to create puzzles for the player to solve.

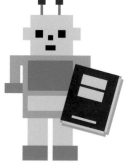

◁ **Rules**

The rules of a game tell you what you're allowed and not allowed to do. For example, can you walk through walls or do they block your path? Can you stop and think or do you have to beat the clock?

**YOU SCORED**

**25,547,010**

**POINTS!!!**

△ **World**

Think about the world in which a game is played. Is it 2D or 3D? Does the player view the game from above, from the side, or from within? Does the game world have walls or boundaries that limit the player's movement or is it open like the outdoors?

△ **Goals**

Every game challenges the player to achieve some kind of goal, whether it's winning a race, conquering an enemy, beating a high score, or simply surviving for as long you can. Most games have lots of small goals, such as unlocking doors to new levels or winning new vehicles or skills.

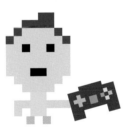

◁ **Controls**

Keyboards, mice, joysticks, and motion sensors all make good controllers. Games are more fun when the player feels in complete control of the character, so the controls should be easy to master and the computer should respond instantly.

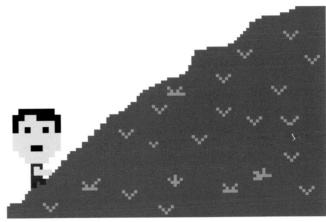

△ **Difficulty level**

A game's no fun if it's too easy or too hard. Many games make the challenges easy at the start, while the player is learning, and more difficult later as the player's skills improve. Getting the difficulty level just right is the key to making a great game.

## GAME DESIGN

## Playability

Games don't have to be complicated to make people want to play them over and over again. One of the first successful computer games was a simple tennis simulator called Pong. The ball was a white square and the racquets were white lines that could only move up and down. Although there were no fancy graphics, people loved Pong because it had great playability. They could compete against friends, just like in real tennis, and it was just hard enough to demand intense concentration and a steady hand, leaving players always wanting another game.

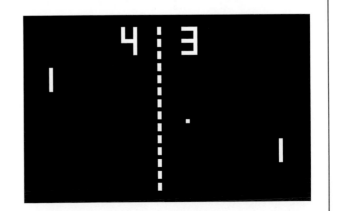

# Types of games

Games come in all shapes and sizes, but most fit into one of just a few main categories, called genres. Some gamers like the platform games genre best, whereas others prefer racing games or strategy games. What are your favorite genres?

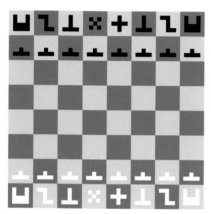

◁ **Traditional**
When you can't find an opponent to play with you, a computer can challenge you to a game of cards, chess, or a million other popular board games.

△ **Role-playing**
Dungeons, dragons, and castles feature in these adventure games. Players may roam freely or follow a set storyline, with their character developing specialized skills as it advances, such as casting spells or sword-fighting. Some role-playing games are played online, allowing lots of players to interact in the same game world.

▷ **Racing**
Racing games create the illusion of speed by making the scenery scroll past the player's viewpoint. To succeed, you need to learn each racetrack inside out so you can start tricky maneuvers in advance.

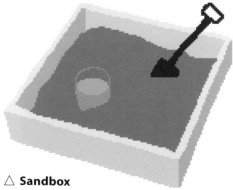

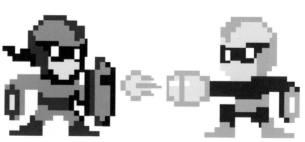

△ **Sandbox**
Some games force players along a set path, but sandbox games are the opposite: they give you complete freedom to explore the game world at your own pace and choose different quests within it.

△ **Combat**
Nimble fingerwork is vital for games involving close-quarters combat. The key to success is knowing when and how to use many different attack and defense moves, from slams and somersaults to special powers.

▷ **Strategy**

Decisions, decisions. What are the best choices to make if you're running a zoo, fighting a war, or building a whole civilization? Strategy games give the player godlike powers over many different characters at once, but you have to manage resources cleverly or your empire will collapse.

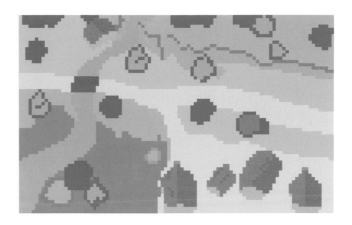

△ **Simulator**

If you want a puppy but don't want the trouble of feeding and walking it, a virtual pet might suit you. Simulators aim to re-create real-life situations. Some are more than just a game: flight simulators are so accurate and realistic that professional pilots use them for training.

◁ **Music and dance**

Dance-mat games involve tapping the feet or jumping over a stream of obstacles in time to the rhythm. Music games allow you to play along with a virtual band using a pretend instrument. You need to hit the right notes on time to complete each level.

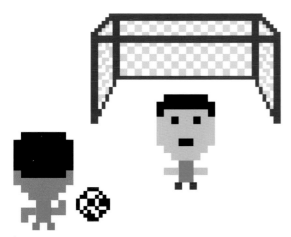

△ **Sport**

Play the game of your choice as your favorite team, set in a realistic stadium with roaring crowds. Sports games let you compete in famous tournaments such as the soccer World Cup, with the computer referee ensuring fair play.

△ **Puzzle**

Some people love to exercise their brains with puzzles. There are many different types, from colorful tile-matching games to number puzzles and escape games, in which you need to use your imagination to find your way from room to room.

# How coding works

A computer can't think for itself—it works by blindly following instructions. It can only carry out a complex task if that task has been broken down into simple steps that tell it exactly what to do and in what order. Writing these instructions in a language a computer understands is called coding.

## Planning a game

Imagine you want to create a game in which you fly a parrot over a river, collecting apples as they drift downstream but avoiding an angry lion. You would need to give the computer a separate set of instructions for each object in the game: the apple, the parrot, and the lion.

The player makes the parrot fly left and right with the left and right arrow keys.

Pressing the space key makes the parrot dive, but the game ends if you touch the lion.

Score  10

The player wins a point each time the parrot gets an apple.

The apple drifts downstream over and over. It reappears on the left if the parrot takes it.

The lion walks left and right, following the parrot.

▽ **Apple**
You can't simply tell the computer that the apple drifts down the river and vanishes when the parrot eats it. Instead, you need to break down this complicated task into a set of very simple steps as shown here.

Jump to the left edge of the screen.

Repeat the following steps over and over again:

Move a bit to the right.

If I get to the right edge of the screen then

jump back to the left edge.

If I touch the parrot then

add one to the parrot's score and

jump back to the left edge.

▷ **Parrot**

The parrot is more complicated than the apple because the player controls it and it can move up, down, left, and right. Even so, it's possible to make all of this work by writing a sequence of simple instructions.

Jump to the top right of the screen.

Repeat these steps in turn:

If the player presses the left arrow then

move a bit to the left if I can.

If the player presses the right arrow then

move a bit to the right if I can.

If the player presses the space key then

move all the way to the bottom of the screen taking a second and

move all the way back to the top taking a second

▷ **Lion**

The lion is the player's enemy and can end the game if the parrot touches it. It is controlled by a simple program.

Jump to the middle of the screen.

Repeat these steps in turn:

If the parrot is to my left then

move a bit to my left.

If the parrot is to my right then

move a bit to my right.

If the parrot touches me then

stop the game.

**LINGO**

## Programming languages

The instructions on this page are in simple English, but if you wanted to create the game on a computer, you would need to translate them into special words that the computer can understand: a programming language. Writing programs with a programming language is called coding or programming. This book uses the programming language Scratch, which is ideal for learning about coding and great for making games.

# Introducing Scratch

The characters and other objects in Scratch games are called sprites.

All the games in this book are made with a programming language called Scratch. Scratch is easy to learn because you don't have to type any complicated code. Instead, you build programs from ready-made blocks.

## Starting from scratch

A project in Scratch usually starts with choosing the objects, or sprites, that will appear in the game. Scratch has a large library of sprites, or you can create your own.

### Sprites

Sprites are the things that move around or react in the game. They can be anything from animals and people to pizzas or spaceships. You can bring each sprite to life on screen with a list of instructions called a script.

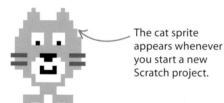

The cat sprite appears whenever you start a new Scratch project.

### Scripts

Scripts are made of text blocks that you can drag with a computer mouse and join like pieces of a jigsaw puzzle. Each block has one instruction so it's easy to understand.

Hello!

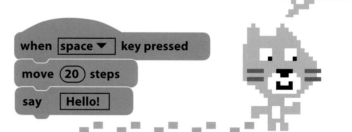

### Working together

Games are usually made up of several sprites working together, each controlled by its own script. Scripts make sprites move around, crash into each other, create sounds, and change color or shape.

Some sprites act as enemies to make a game more difficult.

HELP!

**EXPERT TIPS**

## Experimenting

Scratch is all about experimenting. Once you've built a game, it's easy to add things to it or change how it works by tinkering with the script. You can see the effect of your changes straight away.

# A typical Scratch project

Once you've built a script, you can click the green flag to see what it does. All the action takes place in a part of the Scratch window called the "stage". Sprites move about on the stage, often in front of a background image that helps create atmosphere.

The red button stops a program.

The green flag starts, or runs, the program.

▷ **Running a program**
Starting, or "running", a program activates the scripts that you've built. To make the stage fill your whole computer screen, click the blue symbol in the top left.

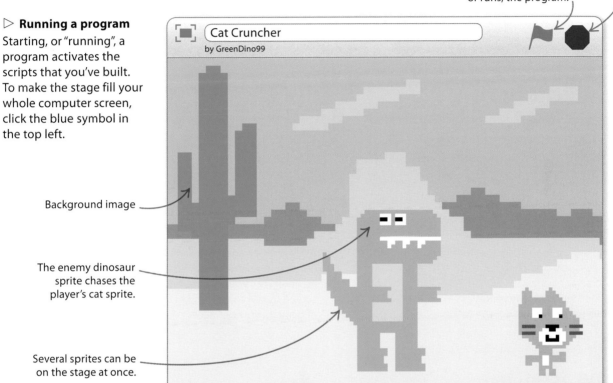

Cat Cruncher
by GreenDino99

Background image

The enemy dinosaur sprite chases the player's cat sprite.

Several sprites can be on the stage at once.

▽ **Making sprites move**
In a typical game, the player moves one sprite and the other sprites are programmed to move automatically. The script below makes the dinosaur in this project chase the cat.

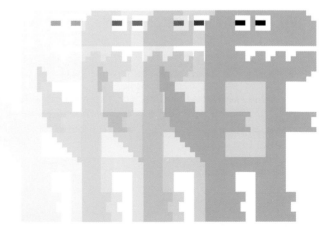

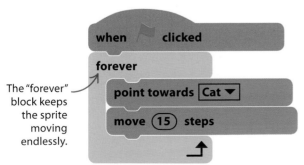

when 🏳 clicked
forever
point towards Cat ▼
move 15 steps

The "forever" block keeps the sprite moving endlessly.

# Getting Scratch

In order to try the projects in this book, you'll need to set up Scratch on a desktop or laptop computer. The two ways of setting up Scratch (online and offline) are shown below.

## Online Scratch

If you have a reliable internet connection, you can run Scratch online in a browser window without downloading anything. You will need to set up a Scratch account.

### 1 Join Scratch

To set up the online version, visit the Scratch website at **scratch.mit.edu** and click "Join Scratch". You will need to set up an account with a username and password. Your games will stay private unless you click "Share", which will publish them on the web.

### 2 Sign in

After you've joined the Scratch website, click "Sign in" and enter your username and password. It's best not to use your real name as your username. Click "Create" at the top of the screen to start a new project. If you use the online version of Scratch, you can access your projects from any computer.

## Offline Scratch

You can also download the Scratch program to your computer so you can use it offline. This is particularly useful if your internet connection is unreliable.

### 1 Install Scratch

For the offline version of Scratch, go to **scratch.mit.edu/scratch2download**. Follow the instructions on screen to download the installation files, then double-click them. After installation, a Scratch icon will appear on your desktop.

### 2 Launch Scratch

Double-click the icon on the desktop and Scratch will open, ready for you to begin programming. There's no need to create a user account if you use the offline version of Scratch.

△ **Operating system**
The online version of Scratch works well on Windows, Ubuntu, and Mac computers, although it won't work on tablets. The offline version of Scratch works well on Windows and Mac computers. If your computer uses Ubuntu, try the online version instead.

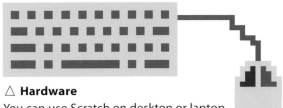

△ **Hardware**
You can use Scratch on desktop or laptop computers, but it's easier if you use a mouse than a touchpad. Scratch apps for tablets and smartphones are also being developed.

◁ **Saving**
If you use Scratch offline, remember to save from time to time. The online version saves automatically. Online, you can undo all the changes you've made since you last opened a project by choosing "Revert" in the File menu.

# Old and new versions

This book is based on Scratch 2.0, the latest version at the time of writing. The projects in this book will not work with older versions of Scratch, so make sure you have 2.0.

▽ **Version 1.4**
In older versions of Scratch, such as Scratch 1.4, the stage is on the right and the scripts area is in the middle.

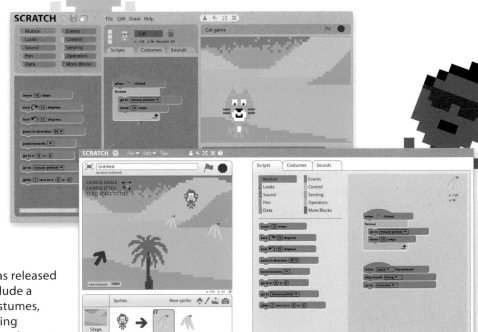

▷ **Version 2.0**
This version of Scratch was released in 2013. New features include a "Backpack" for storing costumes, media, and scripts; a cloning function; a sound editor; and a more sophisticated paint editor.

# Scratch tour

The Scratch window is divided into several different areas. Scripts are built on the right, while the stage on the left shows the game running.

**The stage**
When you play a game or run any other kind of project in Scratch, you see the action happening on the stage, which serves as a miniature screen. You can see changes to your script take effect immediately on the stage simply by clicking the green flag button to run the project.

Switch to full screen view

Change language

Menus

Cursor tools

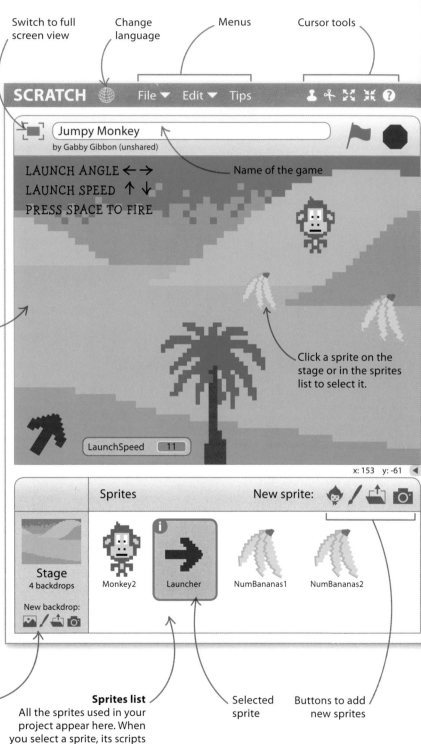

Name of the game

Click a sprite on the stage or in the sprites list to select it.

Selected sprite

Buttons to add new sprites

**Sprites list**
All the sprites used in your project appear here. When you select a sprite, its scripts appear in the scripts area.

Click these icons to change the backdrop image on the stage.

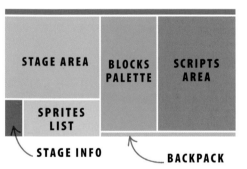

△ **Scratch window**
The stage and sprites list occupy the left of the Scratch window, while script-building areas are on the right. The tabs above the scripts area reveal other Scratch features.

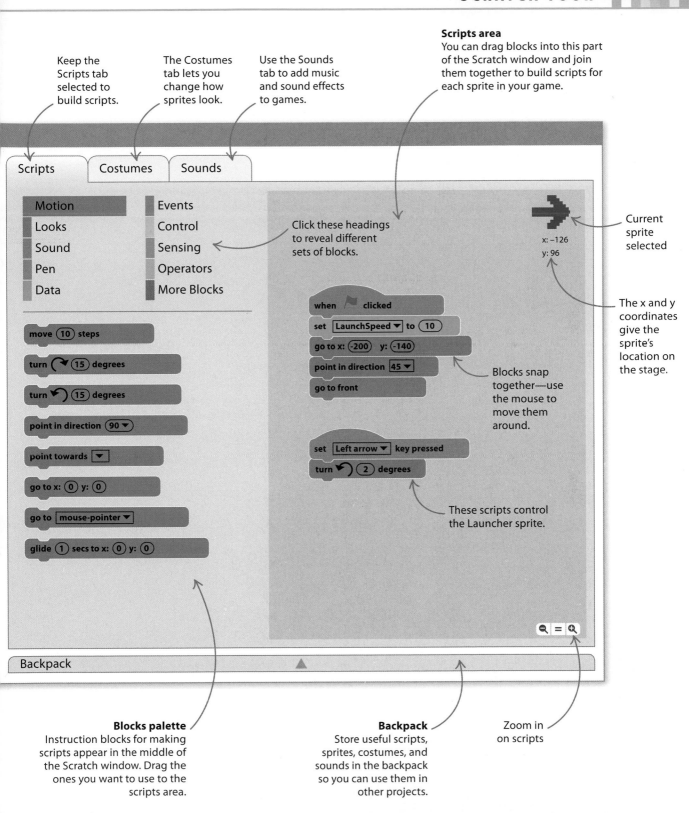

**Scripts area**
You can drag blocks into this part of the Scratch window and join them together to build scripts for each sprite in your game.

Keep the Scripts tab selected to build scripts.

The Costumes tab lets you change how sprites look.

Use the Sounds tab to add music and sound effects to games.

Scripts    Costumes    Sounds

Motion      Events
Looks       Control
Sound       Sensing
Pen         Operators
Data        More Blocks

Click these headings to reveal different sets of blocks.

Current sprite selected

x: −126
y: 96

The x and y coordinates give the sprite's location on the stage.

move (10) steps

turn (15) degrees

turn (15) degrees

point in direction (90 ▼)

point towards (▼)

go to x: (0) y: (0)

go to (mouse-pointer ▼)

glide (1) secs to x: (0) y: (0)

when ⚑ clicked

set (LaunchSpeed ▼) to (10)

go to x: (-200)   y: (-140)

point in direction (45 ▼)

go to front

Blocks snap together—use the mouse to move them around.

set (Left arrow ▼) key pressed

turn (2) degrees

These scripts control the Launcher sprite.

Q = Q

Backpack                    ▲

**Blocks palette**
Instruction blocks for making scripts appear in the middle of the Scratch window. Drag the ones you want to use to the scripts area.

**Backpack**
Store useful scripts, sprites, costumes, and sounds in the backpack so you can use them in other projects.

Zoom in on scripts

# Star
# Hunter

# How to build Star Hunter

Welcome to your first Scratch game: Star Hunter, a fast-paced, underwater treasure hunt. Just follow the simple steps in this chapter to build the game, then challenge a friend to beat your score.

## AIM OF THE GAME

The aim of this game is to collect as many gold stars as you can. Use the cat to collect the stars, but watch out for deadly octopuses. You'll need to move quickly to succeed. The main sprites in the game are shown below.

◁ **Cat**
Move the cat around the screen with your computer mouse—the cat sprite follows the mouse-pointer.

◁ **Octopuses**
The octopuses patrol the seas but they swim more slowly than you. If you touch one, the game is over!

◁ **Stars**
These appear one at a time in random places. Touch a star to score a point.

Click this icon to make the game fill your screen.

Type in the name of your game.

The score shows how many stars you've collected.

Star Hunter
by Octoblaster99 (unshared)

Score    0

An underwater backdrop image sets the scene.

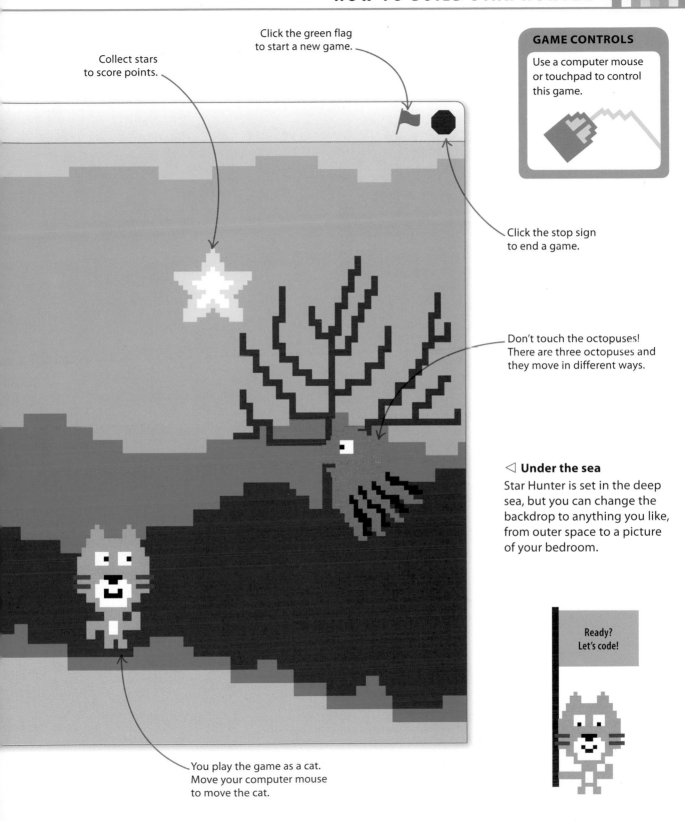

Collect stars
to score points.

Click the green flag
to start a new game.

Click the stop sign
to end a game.

Don't touch the octopuses!
There are three octopuses and
they move in different ways.

◁ **Under the sea**
Star Hunter is set in the deep
sea, but you can change the
backdrop to anything you like,
from outer space to a picture
of your bedroom.

You play the game as a cat.
Move your computer mouse
to move the cat.

Ready?
Let's code!

# Building scripts

Like any Scratch program, Star Hunter is made by joining colored blocks like the pieces of a jigsaw puzzle. Each block is an instruction that tells a sprite what to do. Let's start by programming the game's main sprite: the cat.

**1** Start Scratch and choose either "create" or "New Project". You'll see a screen like the one below, with the cat sprite in place. In the middle is a set of blue instruction blocks.

Clicking the buttons here reveals different sets of blocks.

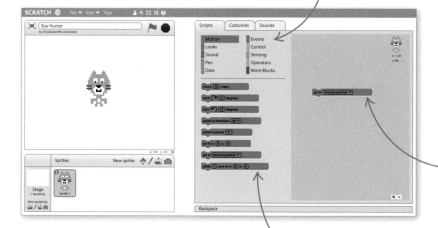

Drag your chosen blocks here to build a script.

Choose blocks from the list in the middle.

**2** We'll program the cat to move wherever the player moves the computer mouse. Click on the "go to mouse-pointer" block and drag it to the right part of the screen—the scripts area.

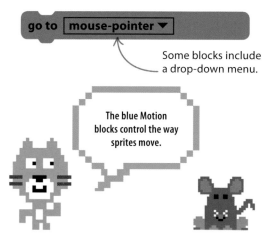

go to mouse-pointer ▼

Some blocks include a drop-down menu.

The blue Motion blocks control the way sprites move.

**3** Now select the yellow Control button and look for a "forever" block.

| Scripts | Costumes | Sounds |
| --- | --- | --- |

Motion     Events
Looks      Control
Sound     Sensing
Pen        Operators
Data      More Blocks

Click Control to reveal the yellow blocks.

wait (10) secs

repeat (10)

forever

Drag the "forever" block to the scripts area.

**4** Drag it to the right and drop it over the blue block. It will wrap around it like this:

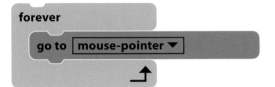

**5** Next, select the brown Events button. Look for a block with a green flag. Drag it to the right and add it to the top of your script. Read through the script and think about what each block does.

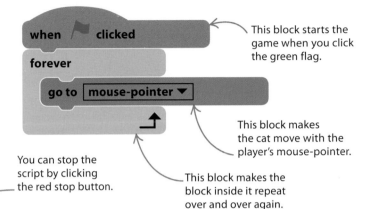

This block starts the game when you click the green flag.

This block makes the cat move with the player's mouse-pointer.

This block makes the block inside it repeat over and over again.

**6** Now look at the top right of the stage—you'll see a green flag. Click this to run your script.

Click the green flag to play.

You can stop the script by clicking the red stop button.

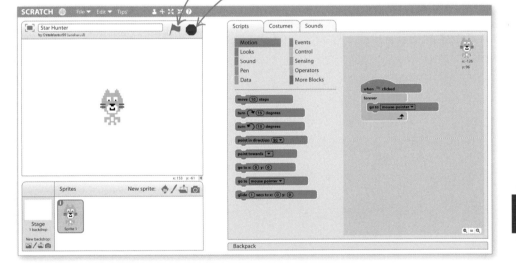

**7** Move your mouse and watch what happens. If you followed all the steps, the cat will move with the mouse-pointer around the stage.

▷ **Well done!**
You have created your first Scratch project. Let's add some more things to the project to build a game.

Bravo!

**8** The cat is called "Sprite1". Let's fix that. In the sprites list, select Sprite1 (the cat) and click on the blue "i" in the corner to get more information about the sprite. Change the name to "Cat".

Type the sprite's name here.

Click here to bring up the information pop-up box.

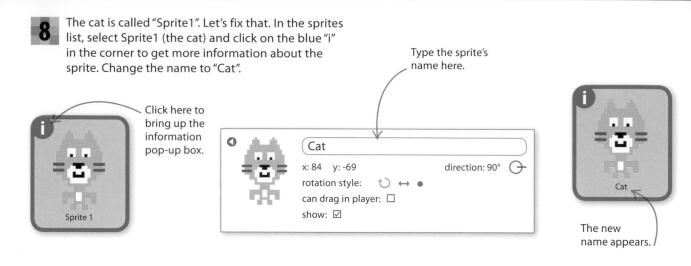

Cat

x: 84    y: -69                                    direction: 90°

rotation style: ↻  ↔  ●

can drag in player: ☐

show: ☑

Sprite 1

Cat

The new name appears.

## Setting the scene

At the moment, the stage is just a boring white rectangle. Let's create some atmosphere by adding scenery and sound effects. To change the scenery, we add a "backdrop" image.

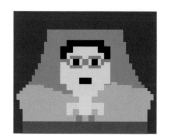

**9** To the left of the sprites list is a button to add a picture from the backdrop library. Click it and look for "underwater2". Select the image and click "OK". The backdrop will now fill the stage.

The backdrop is just decoration and doesn't affect the sprites.

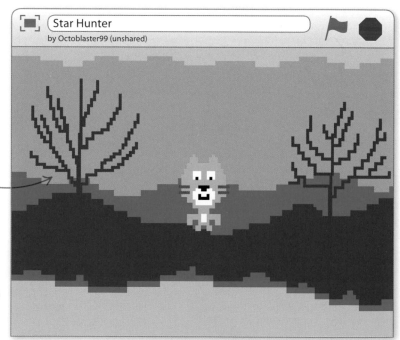

Star Hunter

by Octoblaster99 (unshared)

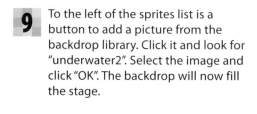

Stage

1 backdrop

New backdrop:

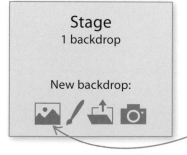

Click this icon to open the backdrop library.

# Sound effects

Now we'll add a bubbling sound to the cat sprite to make it sound like we're underwater.

Delete
sounds here.

**10** Highlight the cat in the sprites list and then click the Sounds tab above the blocks palette. Click the speaker icon to choose a sound from the library.

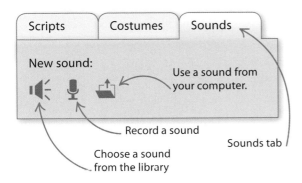

| Scripts | Costumes | Sounds |
|---|---|---|

New sound:

Use a sound from
your computer.

Record a sound

Choose a sound
from the library

Sounds tab

**11** Look for "bubbles" in the library. You can preview sounds by clicking the play symbol. To load a sound into the game, click the speaker icon and then "OK". Now you'll see bubbles in your list of sounds.

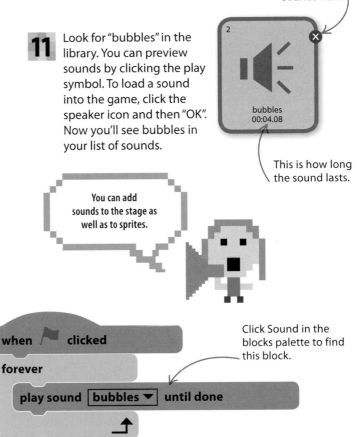

bubbles
00:04.08

This is how long
the sound lasts.

You can add
sounds to the stage as
well as to sprites.

**12** Click the Scripts tab and add the following script to the cat sprite, but leave the old script in place because you need both. The new script repeats the bubbles sound. The "play sound ... until done" block waits for the sound to finish before letting it start again. Run the game to hear the sound effect.

when 🚩 clicked

forever

play sound **bubbles ▼** until done

Click Sound in the
blocks palette to find
this block.

## Loops

A loop is a section of code that repeats over and over again. The "forever" block creates a loop that carries on forever, but other types of loop can repeat an action a fixed number of times. Loops are very common in almost all computer programming languages.

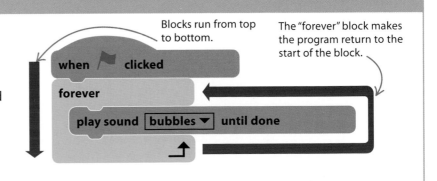

Blocks run from top
to bottom.

The "forever" block makes
the program return to the
start of the block.

when 🚩 clicked

forever

play sound **bubbles ▼** until done

## Add an enemy

The game needs an enemy to make things more interesting. Let's add an octopus with a deadly sting. The octopus will patrol the stage, moving left and right, and the player will have to keep out of its way or the game is over.

**13** To add a second sprite to the project, click the icon shown below to open up the sprite library. Choose the octopus and click "OK".

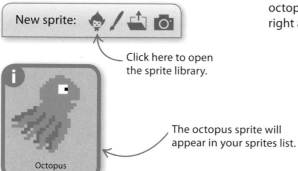

Click here to open the sprite library.

The octopus sprite will appear in your sprites list.

**14** Add the following script to the octopus sprite. To find the blue blocks, click on Motion in the blocks palette. The two Motion blocks used here make the octopus move left and right across the stage.

This block runs the script when the game begins.

Motion blocks are dark blue and control the way sprites move.

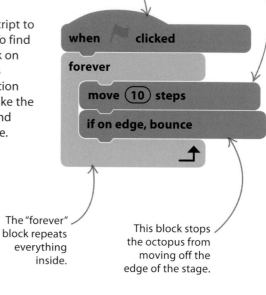

The "forever" block repeats everything inside.

This block stops the octopus from moving off the edge of the stage.

**15** Now run the script. The octopus will patrol left and right, but you'll notice it's upside down half the time. We can fix this by changing the way the sprite turns around when it changes direction. Highlight the octopus and click the blue "i". In the pop-up box, there are three options after "rotation style".

The middle option makes the sprite flip sideways when it bounces.

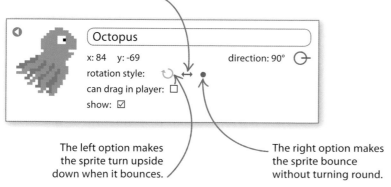

The left option makes the sprite turn upside down when it bounces.

The right option makes the sprite bounce without turning round.

**16** Choose the middle option and run the project. The octopus should now stay right side up and facing forward all the time. You can adjust its starting position on the screen by dragging it with the mouse.

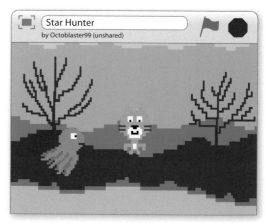

# Collisions

So far the octopus and cat move through each other without anything happening. We need to add a script to make them stop moving when they collide. Collision detection is very important in computer games.

**17** Highlight the octopus and drag a yellow "if then" block to an empty part of the scripts area. Now add a pale blue "touching" block to the top of the "if then" block. Click the drop-down menu and choose "Cat". This script will help the octopus detect the cat.

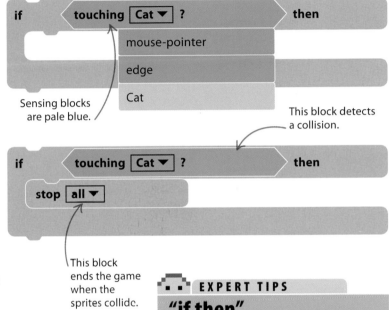

Sensing blocks are pale blue.

This block detects a collision.

**18** Choose Control in the blocks palette again, and add a "stop all" block to the middle of the "if then" block. This will stop all action if the octopus is touching the cat, ending the game.

```
if    touching  Cat ▼  ?    then
   stop  all ▼
```

This block ends the game when the sprites collide.

**19** Now add the "if then" blocks you've built to the octopus's main script, placing it carefully after the blue Motion blocks. Also, add a "wait 0.5 sec" before the loop. Run the project and see what happens.

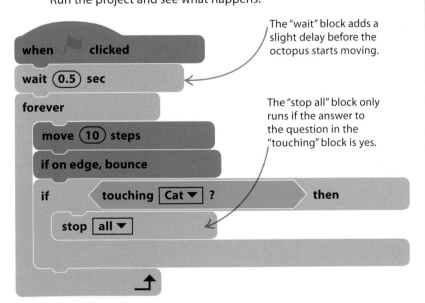

The "wait" block adds a slight delay before the octopus starts moving.

The "stop all" block only runs if the answer to the question in the "touching" block is yes.

## "if then"

You make decisions every day. If it's raining, you might use an umbrella. If it isn't, you don't. Computer programs do the same thing by using what programmers call conditional statements, such as "if then". When Scratch reaches an "if then" block, it runs the blocks inside only if the statement is true.

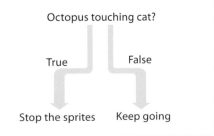

Octopus touching cat?

True          False

Stop the sprites    Keep going

# More enemies

Let's add more enemies to the game, but to make things more challenging, we'll make them move in different directions. We can tell each sprite exactly which way to go by using a block that works like a compass.

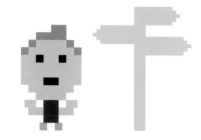

**20** Add a purple "set size" block to the top of the octopus's script, after the "when clicked" block. Set the octopus's size to 35% to make the game a bit easier. Then add a blue "point in direction" block.

**21** To change the octopus's direction, click on the window in the "point in direction" block and type 135 in place of 90. This will make the octopus move diagonally.

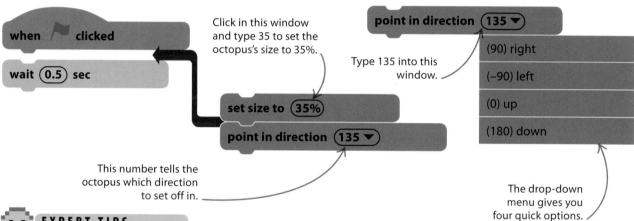

Click in this window and type 35 to set the octopus's size to 35%.

Type 135 into this window.

This number tells the octopus which direction to set off in.

The drop-down menu gives you four quick options.

**• • • EXPERT TIPS**

## Directions

Scratch uses degrees to set direction. You can choose any number from −179° to 180°. Negative numbers point sprites left; positive numbers point them right. Use 0° to go up and 180° to go straight down.

−90° moves a sprite straight to the left.

180° moves a sprite straight down.

**22** Now we can duplicate our octopus to create more enemies. Right-click on the octopus in the sprites list (or control-click if you have a Mac) and choose "duplicate". Copies of the Octopus sprite will appear in the sprites list, named Octopus2 and Octopus3. Each will have a copy of the first octopus's script.

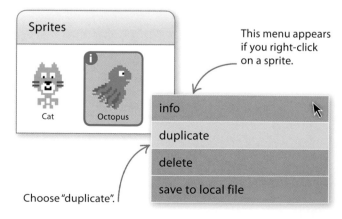

This menu appears if you right-click on a sprite.

Choose "duplicate".

**23** To make the octopuses move in different directions, change the number in the "point in direction" block for each new octopus. Leave the first Octopus sprite's direction as 135, but set Octopus2 to 0 and Octopus3 to 90. Run the project and try to avoid all the enemies.

**24** If it's too hard to stay alive, make the octopuses slower by lowering the number of steps in their "move" blocks to two. Remember to change the script for all three octopus sprites.

Changing this number adjusts the octopus's speed.

```
move (2) steps
if on edge, bounce
```

**25** For more variety, let's make one of the octopuses set off in a random direction. To do this, we use a green "pick random" block. This is Scratch's way of rolling a dice to generate a random number. Choose Operators in the blocks palette to find the block and add it to the first octopus's script. Run the project a few times to see the octopus choose different starting directions.

Type –179 in the first window.

Type 180 in the second window.

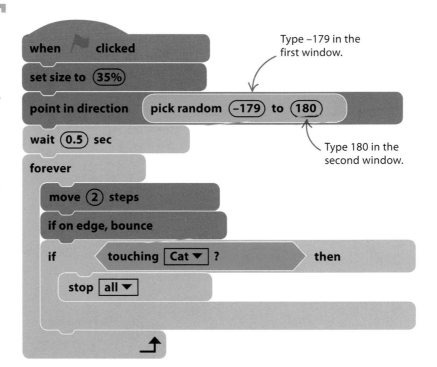

```
when clicked
set size to (35%)
point in direction   pick random (-179) to (180)
wait (0.5) sec
forever
  move (2) steps
  if on edge, bounce
  if    touching [Cat ▼] ?   then
    stop [all ▼]
```

**EXPERT TIPS**
## Random numbers

Why do so many games use dice? Dice create surprises in a game because they make different things happen to each player. A random number is one you can't predict in advance, just like the roll of a dice. You can get the cat to say a random dice roll using this simple code.

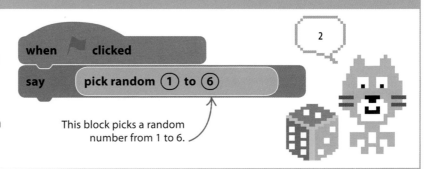

```
when clicked
say   pick random (1) to (6)
```

This block picks a random number from 1 to 6.

# Collecting stars

In many games, the player has to collect valuable items to win points or to stay alive. In Star Hunter, we use gold stars as underwater treasure that the player has to collect. We'll use random numbers again to make each star appear in a new place.

**26** Click the "choose new sprite" symbol ♦ in the sprites list and choose the "Star1" sprite from the library.

Star1

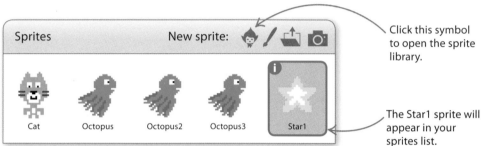

Click this symbol to open the sprite library.

The Star1 sprite will appear in your sprites list.

**27** Add the following script to Star1. This script will make the star move to a random new location whenever the cat touches it. The green blocks create random numbers called coordinates, which Scratch uses to pinpoint locations on the stage.

The "if then" block checks whether the cat is touching the star.

The "go to" block only runs if the answer to the question is yes.

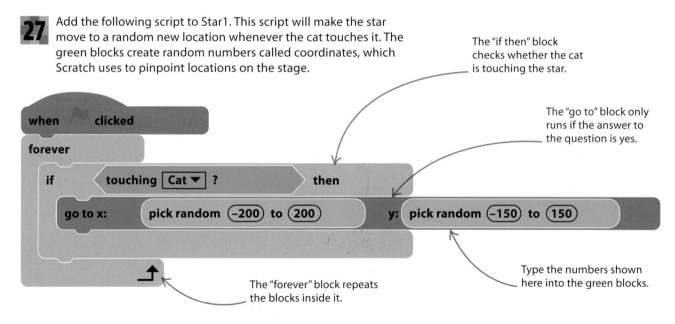

Type the numbers shown here into the green blocks.

The "forever" block repeats the blocks inside it.

**28** To see the star's coordinates change when it moves, choose Motion in the blocks palette and put ticks by "x position" and "y position". Now run the game: you'll see the star's x and y coordinates update each time the cat makes it move. Untick both boxes before you carry on.

Star1: x position  60

Star1: y position  78

## Using coordinates

To pinpoint a location on the stage, Scratch uses numbers called coordinates. These work just like graph coordinates, with x numbers for horizontal positions and y numbers for vertical. To find the coordinates for a spot on the stage, just count the steps across and up from the center of the stage. Positive coordinates are up or right, negative coordinates are down or left. Every spot on the stage has a unique pair of coordinates that can be used to send a sprite to that position.

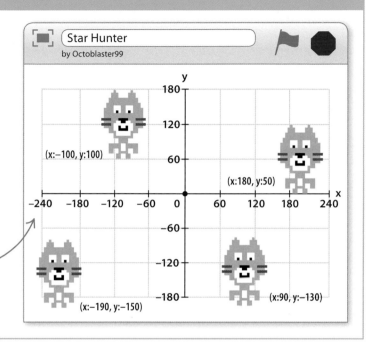

The x axis is longer than the y axis and extends from –240 to 240.

**29** You can add a sound effect that plays when the cat touches a star. First make sure that the star is selected in the sprites list, then click the Sounds tab above the blocks palette. Click the speaker symbol 🔊 to open the sound library. Choose "fairydust" and click "OK". Now add the pink "play sound" block to the star's script and choose "fairydust" in the drop-down list.

Insert the "play sound" block into Star1's existing script, then use the drop-down menu to choose which sound to play.

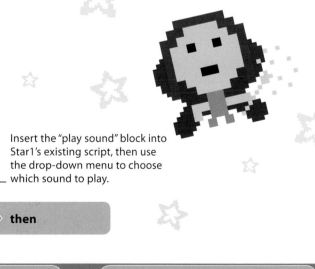

# Keeping score

Computer games often need to keep track of vital statistics such as the player's score or health. We call these changing numbers "variables". To keep track of the player's score in Star Hunter, we'll create a variable that counts the number of stars the player has collected.

**30** With any sprite selected, choose Data in the blocks palette. Click on the button "Make a Variable".

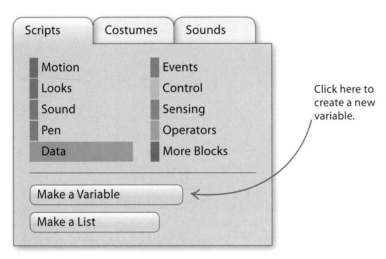

Click here to create a new variable.

**31** A pop-up box appears asking you to give your variable a name. Type "Score" in the box. Make sure the option "For all sprites" is selected and hit "OK".

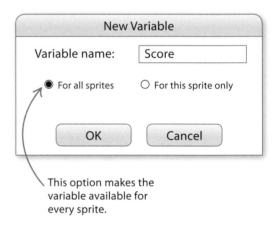

This option makes the variable available for every sprite.

**32** You'll see a new set of blocks appear, including one for the score. Make sure the box next to it is checked to make the score appear on the stage.

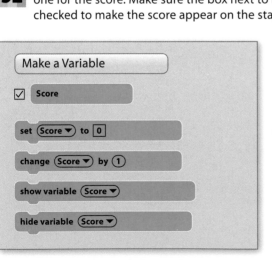

**33** The score counter will appear in the top left of the stage but you can drag it anywhere you like.

You can use the mouse to move the score display.

**34** We want the score to start at zero and increase by one each time the cat touches a star. Select the star sprite and add the two orange Data blocks below to its script.

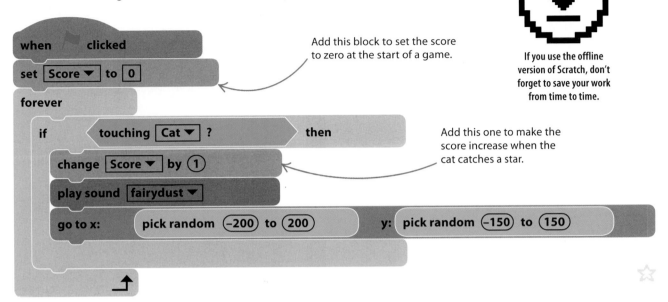

Add this block to set the score to zero at the start of a game.

Add this one to make the score increase when the cat catches a star.

If you use the offline version of Scratch, don't forget to save your work from time to time.

**35** Now click the green flag to run the script and see what happens when the cat collects each star. See if you can collect 20 stars without bumping into an octopus.

 **EXPERT TIPS**

# Variables

A variable works like a box that you can store information in, such as a number than can change. In math, we use letters for variables, such as x and y. In computer programming, we give variables names such as "Score" and use them for storing not just numbers but any kind of information. Try to choose a name that tells you what the variable is for, such as "Speed" or "Score". Most computer languages won't let you put spaces in the names of variables, so a good tip is to combine words. Instead of using "dog speed", for instance, type "DogSpeed".

Hey, I'm X years old!

Big deal, I'm Y years old!

# Better enemies

Now we have a working game, we can test it and experiment with changes that make it easier, harder, or—most important—more fun. One way to make the game more interesting is to make the three octopuses do different things.

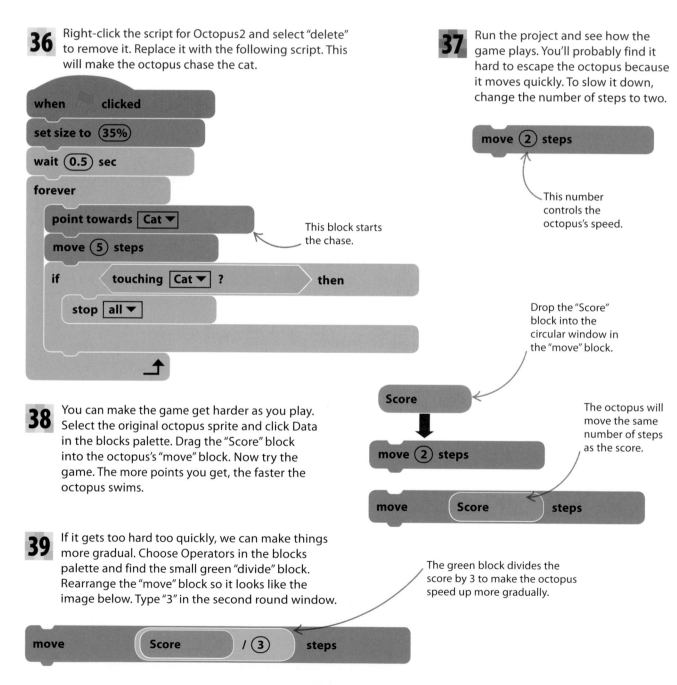

**36** Right-click the script for Octopus2 and select "delete" to remove it. Replace it with the following script. This will make the octopus chase the cat.

when 🏳 clicked

set size to (35%)

wait (0.5) sec

forever

    point towards [Cat ▼]

    move (5) steps

    if ⟨ touching [Cat ▼] ? ⟩ then

        stop [all ▼]

This block starts the chase.

**37** Run the project and see how the game plays. You'll probably find it hard to escape the octopus because it moves quickly. To slow it down, change the number of steps to two.

move (2) steps

This number controls the octopus's speed.

**38** You can make the game get harder as you play. Select the original octopus sprite and click Data in the blocks palette. Drag the "Score" block into the octopus's "move" block. Now try the game. The more points you get, the faster the octopus swims.

Drop the "Score" block into the circular window in the "move" block.

Score

move (2) steps

move (Score) steps

The octopus will move the same number of steps as the score.

**39** If it gets too hard too quickly, we can make things more gradual. Choose Operators in the blocks palette and find the small green "divide" block. Rearrange the "move" block so it looks like the image below. Type "3" in the second round window.

The green block divides the score by 3 to make the octopus speed up more gradually.

move (Score / (3)) steps

**40** Now we'll make Octopus3 patrol in a regular pattern. To do this, we'll use a new Motion block that makes it glide smoothly from point to point, rather than moving in steps. Replace the script for Octopus3 with the following two scripts. These run at the same time, one checking for collisions and the other moving the octopus around its patrol route.

The two scripts are separate in the scripts area.

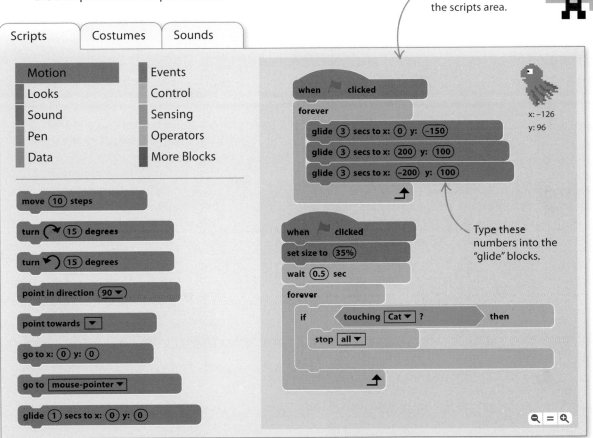

| Scripts | Costumes | Sounds |

Motion
Looks
Sound
Pen
Data

Events
Control
Sensing
Operators
More Blocks

move (10) steps

turn ↻ (15) degrees

turn ↺ (15) degrees

point in direction (90 ▼)

point towards ( ▼)

go to x: (0) y: (0)

go to mouse-pointer ▼

glide (1) secs to x: (0) y: (0)

when ⚑ clicked
forever
　glide (3) secs to x: (0) y: (-150)
　glide (3) secs to x: (200) y: (100)
　glide (3) secs to x: (-200) y: (100)

x: −126
y: 96

when ⚑ clicked
set size to (35%)
wait (0.5) sec
forever
　if ⟨ touching Cat ▼ ? ⟩ then
　　stop all ▼

Type these numbers into the "glide" blocks.

**41** Now run the project and watch Octopus3. It should swim in a repeating triangle pattern.

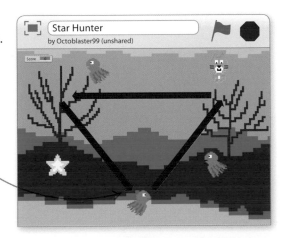

Star Hunter
by Octoblaster99 (unshared)
Score

To change the shape of the triangle, try different numbers in the "glide" blocks.

I feel like I'm swimming in circles...

# Hacks and tweaks

You've built a fun game, but that's just the beginning. Scratch makes it easy to change and adapt games as much as you want. You might find bugs that need fixing, or you might want to make the game harder or easier. Here are some suggestions to get you started.

▽ **Debug Octopus2**

If Octopus2 ends up in the top-right corner at the end of a game, it can trap the player in the next game and end it too quickly. This is a bug. To fix it, you could drag the octopus away from the corner before starting, but it's better to use a script that moves it automatically. Insert a "go to" block at the start of the script for Octopus2 to send it to the center of the stage.

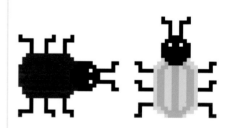

## LINGO

### Bugs

A bug is an error in a program. The first computers made mistakes when real insects, or bugs, got in their circuits. The name stuck. Today, programmers often spend as much time finding and fixing bugs as they do writing code in the first place.

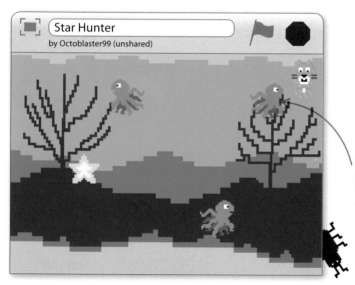

Star Hunter
by Octoblaster99 (unshared)

Octopus2 can trap the player in the top-right corner.

Add this block to make Octopus2 start in the center of the stage.

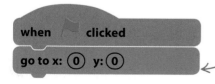

```
when [flag] clicked
go to x: (0) y: (0)
```

△ **Fine-tuning**

The best games have been carefully tested to make sure they play well. Test every change you make and get friends to play your games to see how well they work.

## ▽ Different colors

Make your octopuses different colors by using the "set color" block from the Looks section. Place it under the "set size" block at the start of the script.

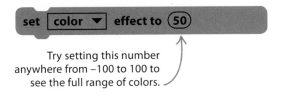

Try setting this number anywhere from –100 to 100 to see the full range of colors.

Hey! Turn me back into a cat!

## △ Scuba diver

To make the underwater theme more convincing, replace the cat with a diver. Click on the cat in the sprites list, then open the Costumes tab and click on the sprite symbol ✿ to open the library. Load the costume called "diver1".

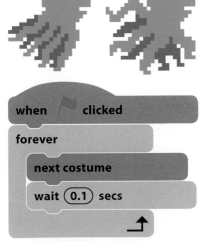

◁ **Swimming animation**

To add a professional touch to Star Hunter, animate the octopuses so that they look as if they're swimming. Add this script to an empty part of the scripts area for each octopus to make them switch between two different poses.

## ▽ Flashing colors

You can make an octopus change color continually to create a flashing effect. Add the script below to any octopus. Try experimenting with different numbers in the "change color" block.

Change this number to make colors change faster or slower.

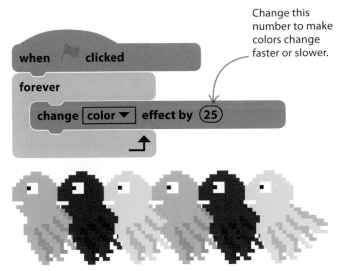

## ▽ Play with size

You can change how easy the game is by adjusting the size of the sprites. Change the number in the octopuses' blue "move" blocks to alter their speed. Change the purple "set size" blocks to make sprites larger or smaller. Fine-tune the numbers until the game is just hard enough to be fun.

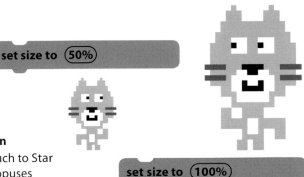

# Cheese Chase

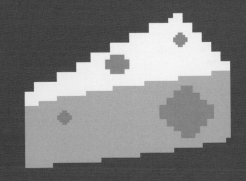

# How to build Cheese Chase

Some of the world's first and most popular computer games were maze games. In a maze game, quick thinking is essential as you race around tight corners, avoiding monsters and collecting treats.

## AIM OF THE GAME

Mimi the mouse is hungry and stuck in a maze. Help her find the cheese but avoid the evil beetles. And watch out for ghosts—the maze is haunted!

◁ **Mimi**
You play the game as the mouse. Use the arrow keys on your keyboard to make her run up, down, left, or right.

◁ **Beetles**
Beetles scuttle along the edges and make random turns when they hit a wall.

◁ **Ghosts**
Ghosts can float through walls. They can appear anywhere without warning and then disappear.

Only the ghosts can move through walls.

Cheese Chase
by SuperMimi (unshared)

Score  30

The beetles are small enough to let the mouse squeeze past.

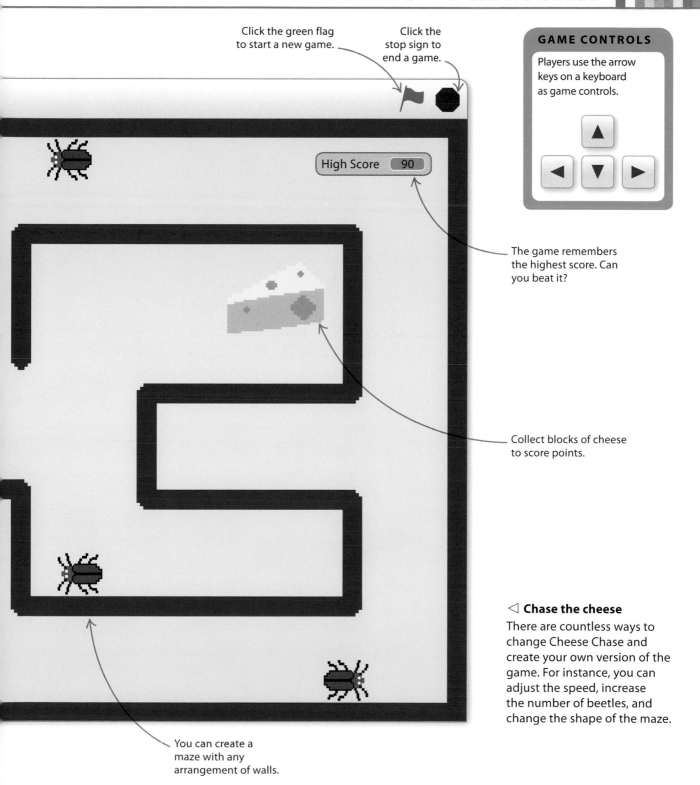

Click the green flag to start a new game.

Click the stop sign to end a game.

**GAME CONTROLS**

Players use the arrow keys on a keyboard as game controls.

High Score    90

The game remembers the highest score. Can you beat it?

Collect blocks of cheese to score points.

◁ **Chase the cheese**
There are countless ways to change Cheese Chase and create your own version of the game. For instance, you can adjust the speed, increase the number of beetles, and change the shape of the maze.

You can create a maze with any arrangement of walls.

# Keyboard control

Many games let the player use the keyboard to control the action. In Cheese Chase, the player uses the arrow keys on the keyboard to move Mimi the mouse around the stage. Start by creating a keyboard control script for Mimi.

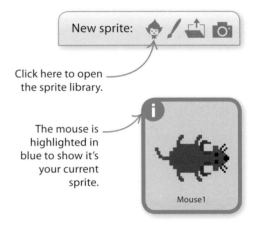

**1** Start Scratch and choose "New Project". Delete the cat by right-clicking and selecting "delete". If you use a Mac computer, instead of right-clicking you can hold down the control key and click.

Sprites

Sprite 1

duplicate

delete

save to local file

hide

**2** Click the "New sprite" symbol and look through the sprite library for Mouse1. Click "OK". The mouse should now be on the stage and in the sprites list.

New sprite:

Click here to open the sprite library.

The mouse is highlighted in blue to show it's your current sprite.

Mouse1

**3** Add this script to the mouse to move the sprite up the stage using the up arrow key. To find the different-colored blocks, remember to click the different options in the Scripts tab. Read through the script carefully and think about what it does. Run the script by clicking the green flag. You should be able to move the Mouse sprite up the stage using the up arrow key.

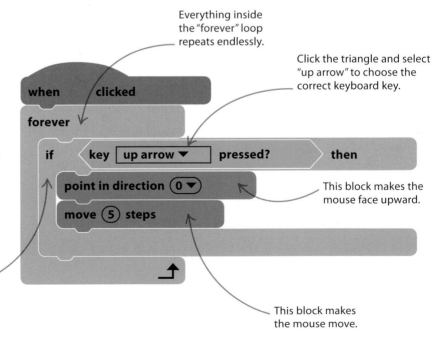

Everything inside the "forever" loop repeats endlessly.

Click the triangle and select "up arrow" to choose the correct keyboard key.

when [ clicked

forever

if [ key [ up arrow ▼ ] pressed? ] then

point in direction (0 ▼)

move (5) steps

This block makes the mouse face upward.

The blocks inside the "if then" block only run when the answer to the question is yes.

This block makes the mouse move.

**4** To make the other arrow keys work, add three more "if then" blocks like the first one, but choose a different arrow key and direction for each one. To move right, select the right arrow key and set the direction to 90. For down, set it to 180. For left, set it to –90. Read through the finished script to make sure you understand it.

Each "if then" block should be inside the "forever" loop, but not inside any of the other "if then" blocks.

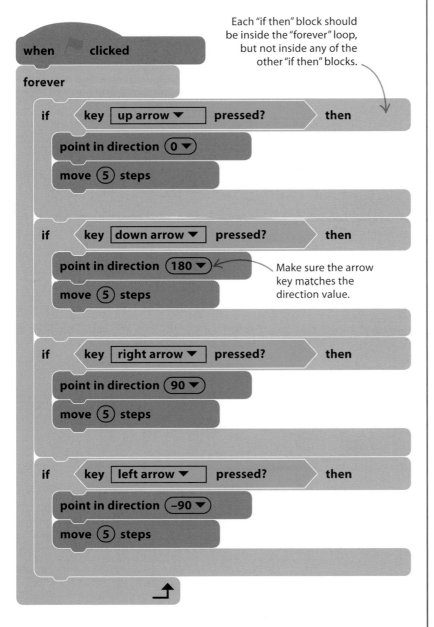

Make sure the arrow key matches the direction value.

**5** Now click the green flag to run the script. You should be able to move the mouse in all directions around the stage using the arrow keys. If it's not working, go back and check all the steps.

**GAME DESIGN**
# Controllers

In Cheese Chase, we use the arrow keys to control the game, and in Star Hunter we used the mouse. Other computer games use very different types of controller.

▷ **Console controller**

Console controllers usually have two small joysticks controlled with your thumbs, along with a range of other buttons. They are ideal for complex games that need a lot of different controls.

▷ **Dance mats**

You control the game by stepping on giant keys. Dance mats are good for games involving physical activity, but they don't give fine control.

▷ **Motion sensor**

These controllers detect movement, which makes them ideal for sports games where you swing your arms to use a racquet or bat, for example.

▷ **Camera**
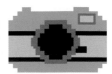
Special cameras in some game consoles allow the player to use body movements to control the game.

# Using the paint editor

Cheese Chase now has its mouse heroine and she's hungry, but there's no cheese yet for her to chase. The sprite library in Scratch doesn't include a picture of cheese, so you'll need to make one yourself. You can do this with Scratch's paint editor.

My cheese piece is a masterpiece!

Use this tool to set the center of the sprite.

**6** Create a blank sprite by clicking the small paintbrush symbol above the sprites list. This will open Scratch's paint editor in a screen like the one below. Make sure that "Bitmap Mode" is selected at the bottom.

Undo

Redo

Crop

Flip

costume1    Clear    Add    Import

Paintbrush tool

Straight line tool

Use this tool to fill a shape with color.

Rectangle tool

Circle tool

Use this tool to select part of a drawing.

Eraser

Use this tool to duplicate part of a drawing.

Outline    Solid    Color palette

Line thickness

Bitmap Mode

Convert to vector

100%

**7** Now draw the cheese. Use the paintbrush tool and choose black from the color palette at the bottom of the screen. Draw the outline of the cheese. If you want perfectly straight lines, use the line tool. Your cheese drawing might be too big at first, but you can make it smaller later.

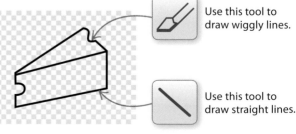

Use this tool to draw wiggly lines.

Use this tool to draw straight lines.

**8** If you like, use the circle tool to draw holes in the cheese. Make the circle an outline rather than a solid circle by choosing the outline option at the bottom.

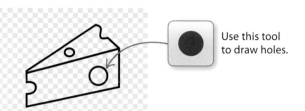

Use this tool to draw holes.

**9** To add color, choose yellow and use the fill tool to fill in the cheese. If your color spills out and fills the whole background, click on the "undo" button. Make sure your lines don't have any gaps, then try again.

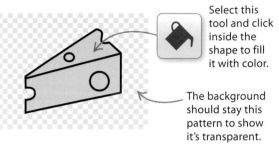

Select this tool and click inside the shape to fill it with color.

The background should stay this pattern to show it's transparent.

**10** Now set the center of your cheese. Click the "Set costume center" tool in the top right and then click the middle of the cheese. The cheese is now ready to be added to the game.

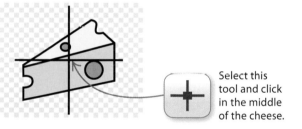

Select this tool and click in the middle of the cheese.

**11** To keep score, we need to create a variable called "Score". Choose Data in the blocks palette and click on "Make a Variable". Type the word "Score" in the pop-up box. The score counter will now appear on the stage.

Score   0

This shows the number in the "Score" variable.

**12** Now add a script to make the cheese appear in a random location. When the mouse touches it, there will be a "pop" noise, the player will score ten points, and the cheese will move to a new location. Run the script and try catching the cheese. It should be easy—but that's because you haven't added enemies yet...

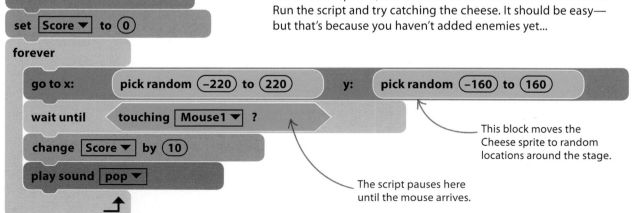

This block moves the Cheese sprite to random locations around the stage.

The script pauses here until the mouse arrives.

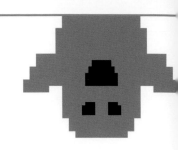

# Getting spooky

Adding our first enemy to the project will make Cheese Chase into a proper game. A ghost is a good first enemy for this game because it can float through walls, so you won't need to change the ghost's script when we add the maze.

**13** Click the "New sprite" symbol and select a ghost sprite from the sprite library. Click "OK" to add it to the project.

Click here to open the library.

Ghost1

The ghost is now your selected sprite.

**14** Add the following script to the ghost to make it chase the mouse. If it touches the mouse, the game will end. You might recognize most of this code from Star Hunter.

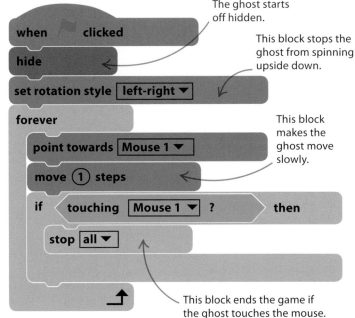

The ghost starts off hidden.

This block stops the ghost from spinning upside down.

This block makes the ghost move slowly.

This block ends the game if the ghost touches the mouse.

Starts a new script. Ghost1 will now have two scripts.

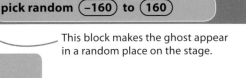

This block keeps the ghost hidden for 5–10 seconds.

This block makes the ghost appear in a random place on the stage.

This block keeps the ghost on screen for 3–6 seconds.

**15** Now add a separate script to make the ghost appear and disappear for random amounts of time. The "hide" block makes the sprite disappear, and "show" makes it appear again.

**16** Next, add music to the game. We usually add music to the stage rather than a sprite. Click the stage area on the left of the sprites list to highlight it in blue. Click the Scripts tab and add the following script to play a sound over and over. Click "Sound" in the blocks palette to find the "play sound until done" block.

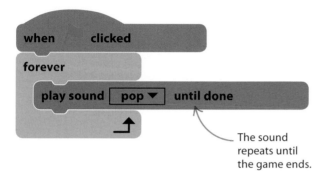

The sound repeats until the game ends.

**17** Now click the Sounds tab above the blocks palette. Click the speaker symbol to open the sound library. Select the category "Music Loops" on the left, then choose the music "xylo1" and click "OK". Repeat the process to load "dance celebrate" into the game too.

Sounds tab

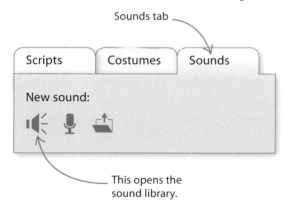

This opens the sound library.

**18** Return to the Scripts tab and change the selected sound from "pop" to "xylo1". Run the game and think about how it feels to play. Next try the sound "dance celebrate". Which one is better?

Click the triangle to choose the sound.

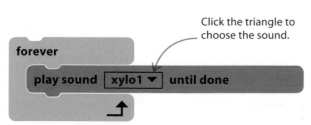

You never know where I'll appear next!

# Making mazes

Mimi the mouse can run anywhere she likes on the stage. Put a stop to that by adding a maze. The maze will make it difficult for her to move from one place to another, adding an extra challenge to Cheese Chase.

ENTER MAZE HERE

This opens the paint editor.

**19** The maze will be a sprite, not a backdrop, because that makes it easier to detect when another sprite touches it. Draw it in Scratch's paint editor. Click on the paintbrush symbol in the sprites list, then click on the blue "i" and rename the sprite "Maze".

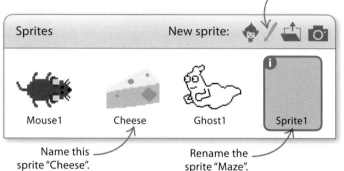

Name this sprite "Cheese".

Rename the sprite "Maze".

**20** Now you can start using the paint editor. Make sure "Bitmap Mode" is selected in the bottom right. If not, click the "Convert to bitmap" button to change the mode. Choose the line tool and set the line width control to the middle. Then pick a dark color for the maze walls.

Draw the maze in the empty space here.

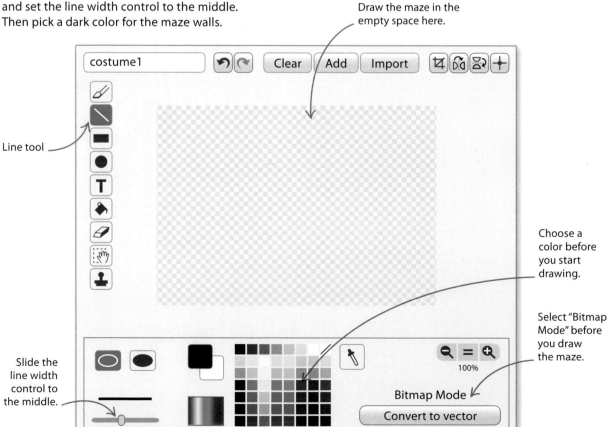

Line tool

Slide the line width control to the middle.

Choose a color before you start drawing.

Select "Bitmap Mode" before you draw the maze.

Bitmap Mode

Convert to vector

**21** Now draw the maze. Start by drawing the outside of the maze at the outer edge of the checkered drawing area. Hold down the shift key on your keyboard to make sure lines are perfectly vertical or horizontal. Then add the inside walls.

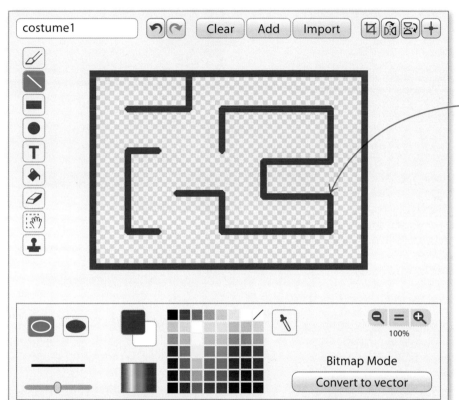

Make sure that the lines of the maze are perfectly straight.

**22** Finally, we need to add a script to make sure the maze is always in the center of the stage so it's fully visible. With the Maze sprite selected, click on the Scripts tab and add the following script.

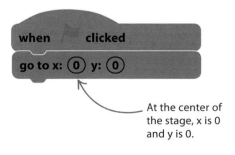

At the center of the stage, x is 0 and y is 0.

**23** Run the project. You'll find that Mimi can run through walls, but don't worry because we'll fix that later.

**24** Mimi, the ghost, and the cheese are all too big for the maze, so we need to shrink them. Add the following blocks at the beginning of Mimi's script, before the "forever" block, and fill in the numbers below.

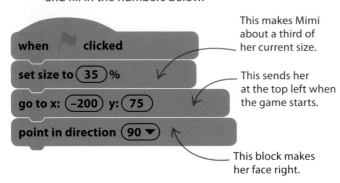

This makes Mimi about a third of her current size.

This sends her at the top left when the game starts.

This block makes her face right.

**25** Now add a purple "set size to" block to the ghost's main script. Set the size to 35 percent. Add a "set size to" block to the Cheese sprite too, and adjust the percentage until the cheese is about twice the size of Mimi.

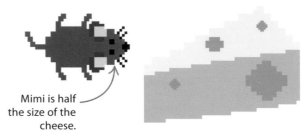

Mimi is half the size of the cheese.

**26** You might need to fine-tune your Maze costume to make sure Mimi can fit through all the passages with enough room to pass her enemies (which we're going to add later). To alter the maze, select the Maze sprite and click the Costumes tab. Use the eraser tool 🧽 to remove walls or the selection tool 🖐 to move them.

Passages should be wide enough for Mimi to pass her enemies.

**27** If you use the eraser, be careful not to leave any flecks of paint behind because Mimi will stop if she hits them. Check the corners of the maze for bumps that Mimi might get stuck on and remove them.

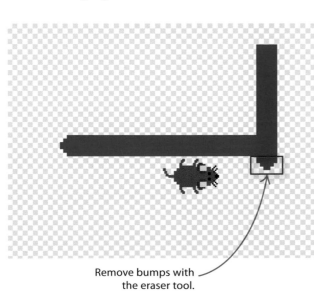

Remove bumps with the eraser tool.

**28** Add a background color to the game by painting a backdrop, not the Maze sprite. At the bottom left of the screen, click the paintbrush symbol in the stage info area. This opens the paint editor. Make sure "Bitmap Mode" is selected at the bottom.

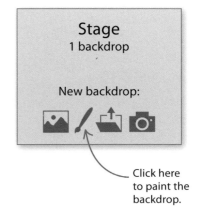

Click here to paint the backdrop.

**29** Choose a color, select the fill tool ◆, and then click on the backdrop to fill it with color.

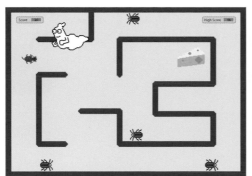

Try different colors to see which one looks best in the maze.

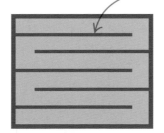

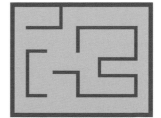

**GAME DESIGN**

# Space in games

How the obstacles in a game are laid out has a big effect on how you play. A maze is the perfect obstacle to demonstrate this.

Walls restrict movement.

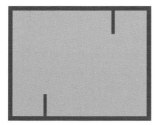

△ **Open space**
The player can move in any direction most of the time. A game like this needs fast-moving enemies or lots of enemies to make it challenging.

△ **Closed-in space**
The player is forced to move in a very limited way. Just one enemy patrolling the corridors of this maze would make life hard. The player has to think ahead to avoid getting trapped.

△ **Balanced space**
This is what the maze in Cheese Chase is designed to be. It limits the player's movement enough to make the game interesting, but allows some freedom.

# Mousetrap

Mimi can currently run straight through the walls of
the maze like a ghost, but we want her to stay trapped
inside the passages. Time to change her script.

Uh oh!

**30** Select Mimi and drag the following blocks to an empty part of the scripts area. This set of blocks will make Mimi reverse if she runs into a wall.

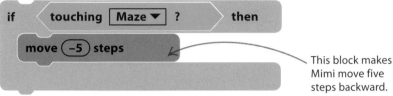

This block makes Mimi move five steps backward.

**31** Insert the blocks four times into Mimi's main script. To make copies, right-click (or control-click if you use a Mac) on the new blocks and select "duplicate". Place the duplicates after each "move 5 steps" block.

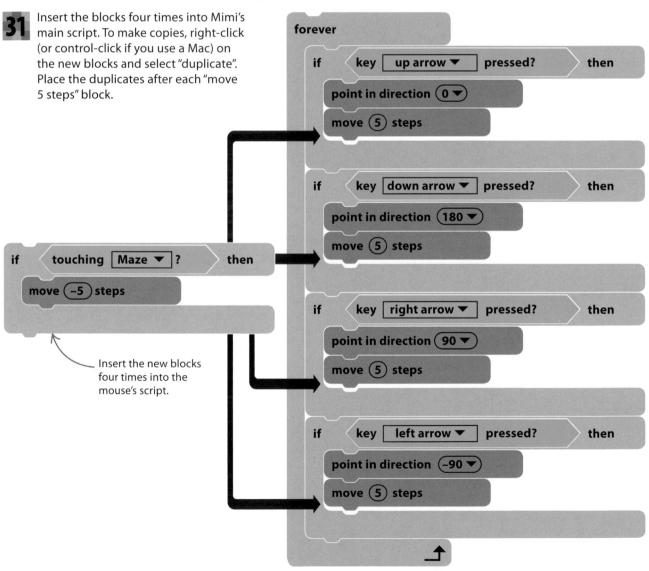

Insert the new blocks four times into the mouse's script.

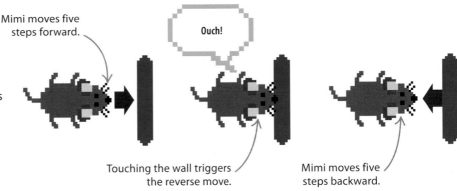

Mimi moves five steps forward.

Ouch!

Touching the wall triggers the reverse move.

Mimi moves five steps backward.

▷ **How does it work?**

You might wonder why Mimi has to move five steps backward. The reason is that she normally moves forward five steps at a time. The backward move reverses the forward one, making her stand still. This happens so quickly that you don't see her reverse.

**32** If Mimi's tail or paws touch a wall when she turns around, she can get stuck. We can fix this bug by making some changes to Mimi's costume in the paint editor.

If Mimi's tail overlaps the wall, she might stop moving.

**34** There's another problem that we can fix. Every sprite has a center point, but if this isn't in the exact center, the mouse will wobble when its direction changes and might overlap a wall and get stuck. Choose the "Set costume center" tool and then click in the exact middle of Mimi to correct her center point.

**33** Select Mouse2 in the sprites list and click the Costumes tab above the blocks palette. Choose "Convert to bitmap" at the bottom, and then use the eraser tool to trim Mimi's tail.

## Bounding boxes

One of the big challenges that game programmers face is detecting when sprites with complicated shapes collide. Even in simple 2D games, collision detection can cause problems, such as sprites getting stuck or solid objects merging. A common solution is to use "bounding boxes"—invisible rectangles or circles that surround the sprite. When these simple shapes intersect, a collision is detected. In 3D games, spheres or 3D boxes can do the same job.

Set costume center

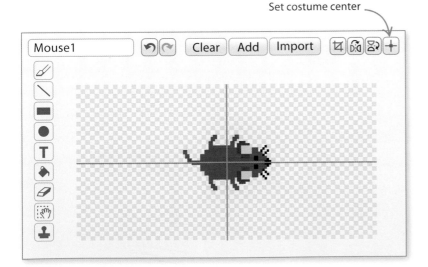

Mouse1 | Clear | Add | Import

# Beetle mania

Now for Mimi's main enemies: a small army of evil beetles that scurry around inside the maze. If she bumps into one, the game ends.

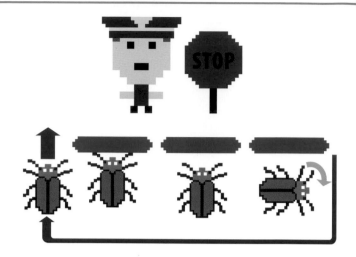

**35** To make the beetles move automatically, you need to create a sequence of steps for them to follow. Programmers call this an algorithm. Our algorithm will tell each beetle to move forward until it hits a wall. Then it will stop, turn, and move forward again.

**36** Click the "New sprite" symbol and choose the Beetle sprite from the library.

The beetle is now your selected sprite.

Beetle

**37** Add the following script to set the beetle's size, location, and direction. It uses a "forever" loop to move the beetle, and an "if then" block to make it stop and turn right whenever it hits a wall.

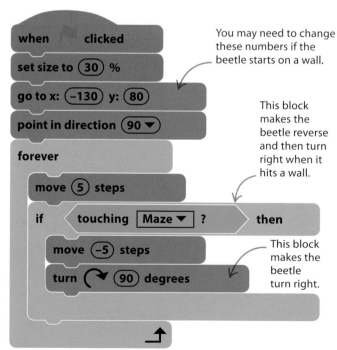

```
when ⚑ clicked
set size to (30) %
go to x: (-130) y: (80)
point in direction (90 ▼)
forever
    move (5) steps
    if  touching Maze ▼ ?  then
        move (-5) steps
        turn ↻ (90) degrees
```

You may need to change these numbers if the beetle starts on a wall.

This block makes the beetle reverse and then turn right when it hits a wall.

This block makes the beetle turn right.

**38** Run the script. You might notice a glitch: the beetle always turns right and ends up going around in loops. We need to change the script so that the beetle turns left or right at random. To make a random choice, use a "pick random" block. Drag it to an empty part of the scripts area and set the second number to 2.

Type "2" here

1

**pick random (1) to (2)**

Click the "pick random" block. You'll see "1" or "2" appear in a speech bubble at random.

**39** Now drag the "pick random" block into the first window of an "equal to" block. Then drag the "equal to" block into an "if then else" block.

This is an "equal to" block.

```
if  ⬡  then

else
```

[ ] = [1]

Type "1" in this window.

**pick random (1) to (2)**

**40** Add two "turn 90 degrees" blocks to make the beetle turn left or right. Read through the script carefully and see if you can figure out how it works.

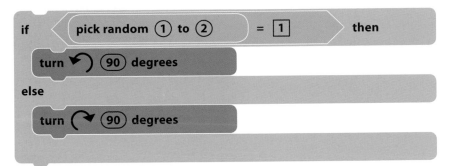

```
if    pick random (1) to (2)  = [1]    then
    turn ↰ (90) degrees
else
    turn ↱ (90) degrees
```

**41** Remove the "turn 90 degrees" block from the beetle's original script and put the "if then else" block in its place, as below. Run the project and watch what happens. Check there's enough room for Mimi to squeeze past the beetle. If not, adjust the maze in the paint editor.

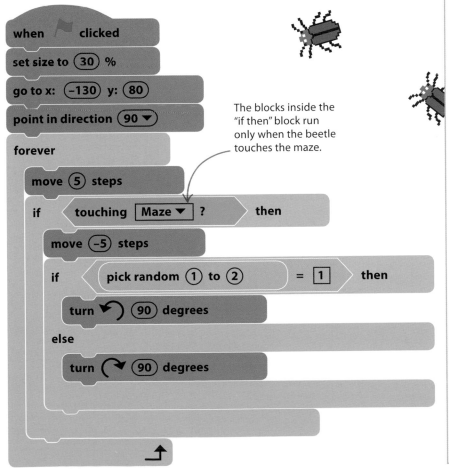

```
when ⚑ clicked
set size to (30) %
go to x: (-130) y: (80)
point in direction (90 ▼)
forever
    move (5) steps
    if    touching [Maze ▼] ?    then
        move (-5) steps
        if    pick random (1) to (2)  = [1]    then
            turn ↰ (90) degrees
        else
            turn ↱ (90) degrees
```

The blocks inside the "if then" block run only when the beetle touches the maze.

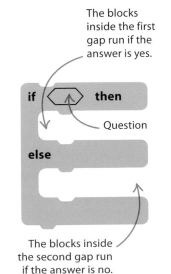

**EXPERT TIPS**

## if then else

The "if then else" block is just like an "if then" but with an extra trick. A normal "if then" asks a question and runs the blocks inside only if the answer is yes. The "if then else" block can hold two groups of blocks: one to run if the answer is yes, and another if the answer is no. The words "if", "then", and "else" are used in nearly all computer languages to make decisions between two options.

The blocks inside the first gap run if the answer is yes.

```
if  ⬡  then


else


```

Question

The blocks inside the second gap run if the answer is no.

## Sending messages

The next step is to make the beetle end the game if Mimi bumps into it. Instead of using another "touching" block in Mimi's script, you can use a message. Scratch lets you send messages between sprites to trigger scripts. The beetle will send a message to Mimi that stops her script.

I have a message for you...

**42** Add the "if then" blocks shown below to the beetle's script. The new blocks check whether the beetle is touching Mimi and, if it is, send a message. Select "Mouse1" in the "touching" block.

```
when   clicked
set size to (30) %
go to x: (−130) y: (80)
point to direction (90 ▼)
forever
    move (5) steps
    if      touching | Maze ▼ | ?        then
        move (−5) steps
        if      pick random (1) to (2)  = 1    then
            turn ↺ (90) degrees
        else
            turn ↻ (90) degrees
```

**43** Now give the message a name. Select "message1" in the "broadcast" block, choose "new message", and type "GameOver".

broadcast | message1 ▼ |
      message1
      new message...

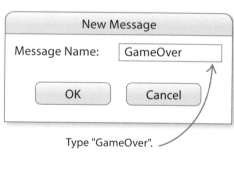

New Message

Message Name:  GameOver

OK          Cancel

Type "GameOver".

Select "Mouse1".

```
if      touching | Mouse1 ▼ | ?        then
    broadcast | message 1 ▼ |
```

This block is found under Events. It sends a message when the beetle hits Mimi.

**44** Now add an extra script to Mimi to receive the message. Drag the following blocks to an empty part of her scripts area. Try the game out. Mimi should stop moving when she touches the beetle, but the beetle will continue to move. Later we'll use a message to show a "GAME OVER!" sign as well.

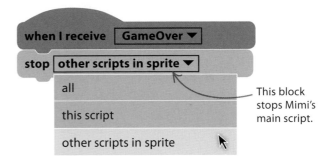

This block stops Mimi's main script.

**45** The game needs more beetles. Copy the Beetle sprite by right-clicking on it (use control-click if you work on a Mac) and then choose "duplicate". Make three new beetles. These will all have the same script. See what happens when you run the project.

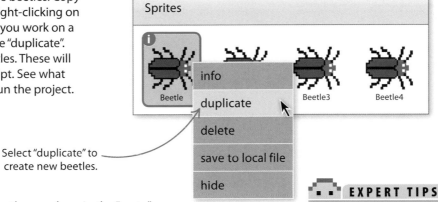

Select "duplicate" to create new beetles.

**46** You'll need to change the numbers in the "go to" blocks for each new beetle so they don't all start in the same place. Starting in different corners works quite well. Experiment!

Beetles start in corners.

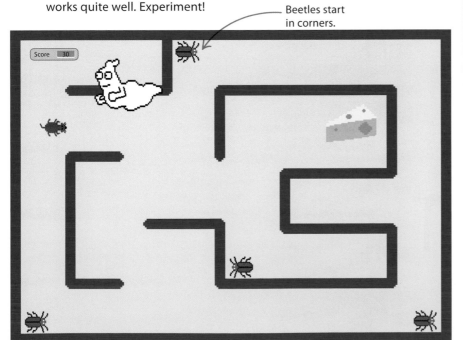

**EXPERT TIPS**

## Messages

Messages provide a neat way of making sprites react to each other. We could have made the mouse check if it's touching a beetle, but that would mean adding "if then" and "touching" blocks to Mimi's script for all four beetles. By using messages, we can add more enemies without changing Mimi's code.

# High score

You can make a game more fun by adding a high score for players to beat. We create this in the same way as the score tracker: by making a variable and displaying it on the stage.

**47** Select Data in the blocks palette. Click "Make a Variable" and create a new variable called "High Score". A new block will appear, and the high score counter will appear on the stage. Drag it wherever you like.

New Variable

Variable name: High Score

● For all sprites    ○ For this sprite only

OK    Cancel

**48** Now add an extra set of blocks to the Cheese sprite's "forever" loop to test for a new high score each time the player gains points. Run the project and see if anyone can beat your high score.

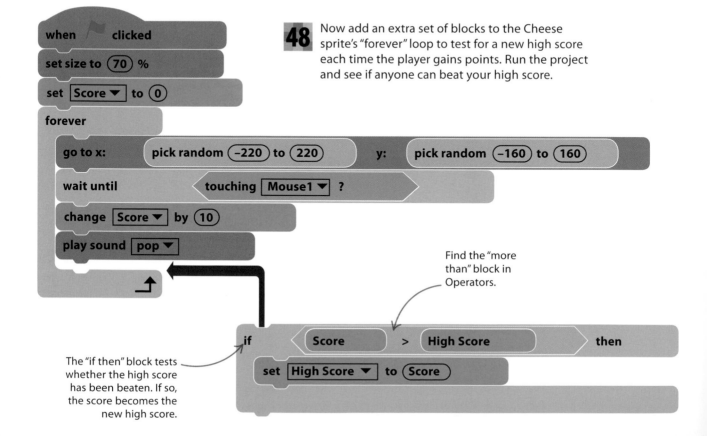

when 🏳 clicked

set size to (70) %

set [Score ▼] to (0)

forever

   go to x: (pick random (–220) to (220))  y: (pick random (–160) to (160))

   wait until < touching [Mouse1 ▼] ? >

   change [Score ▼] by (10)

   play sound [pop ▼]

Find the "more than" block in Operators.

if < (Score) > (High Score) > then

   set [High Score ▼] to (Score)

The "if then" block tests whether the high score has been beaten. If so, the score becomes the new high score.

# Game over!

At the moment, the only signal the game has ended is that the mouse stops moving. You can add a finishing touch to any game by displaying a large, bold "GAME OVER!" sign. To do this you need to create a "Game Over!" sprite and use the "GameOver" message to make it appear.

Don't forget to check the sprite's center with the set center tool.

**49** Click the paintbrush symbol ✎ in the sprites list to create a new sprite with the paint editor. Using "Bitmap Mode", draw a rectangle and fill it with a dark color. Now switch to "Vector Mode". Choose a bright color and use the text tool to type "GAME OVER!" in the rectangle. Change the font to "Scratch" and use the selection tool to make the text large.

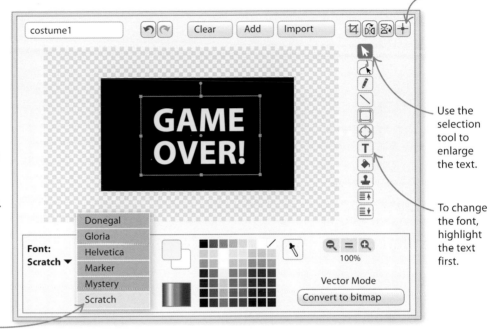

Use the selection tool to enlarge the text.

To change the font, highlight the text first.

Change the font to Scratch.

**50** You don't want the "GAME OVER!" sign to show until the game is really over, so let's hide it with a script. Switch to the Scripts tab and add these blocks.

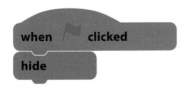

**51** Now add a script to make the sprite appear when the game ends. You can use the same message that stops Mimi to trigger this script.

This places the "GAME OVER!" sign in the middle.

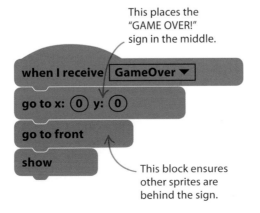

This block ensures other sprites are behind the sign.

**52** Run the game. You should now see the "GAME OVER!" sign when you get caught by a beetle. To make the sign work with the ghost too, replace its "stop all" block with a "broadcast GameOver" block.

# Hacks and tweaks

Take Cheese Chase to the next level by tweaking the rules of the game and the way the sprites behave. You can also experiment with big changes that turn Cheese Chase into a totally different kind of game.

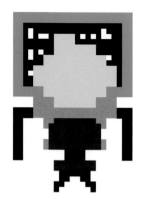

◁ **Play on**

You need to play the game a lot to find out what works and what can be improved. Get other people to play. You can adjust many properties of the game until you get the right configuration: a game where the abilities of the player and enemies are well balanced.

△ **Add sounds**

Jazz up the game with some sound effects using the "play sounds" block when the ghost appears, when the game ends, or when you get a high score. There are lots of sounds in Scratch's sound library that you can experiment with.

▷ **Tweak timings**

You might find Cheese Chase harder than Star Hunter. To make it easier, you can make the beetles slower or make the ghost appear for a shorter time. You can also speed up Mimi. For variety, try making each beetle run at a different speed.

▷ **Rocket power**

Add a power boost that hides all the enemies for ten seconds when the mouse touches it. To do this, you would need to add a new sprite and a message to trigger a hide-wait-show script in each enemy.

▽ **Vanishing cheese**

For an extra challenge, make the cheese spend only ten seconds or so in each spot before moving to a new location. This will force the player to move fast. To do this, give the cheese an extra script with a "forever" loop containing a "wait 10 secs" block, followed by a copy of the "go to" block from the main script.

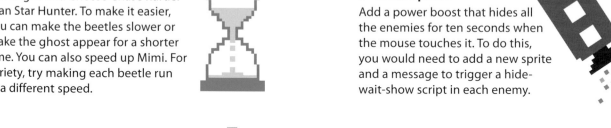

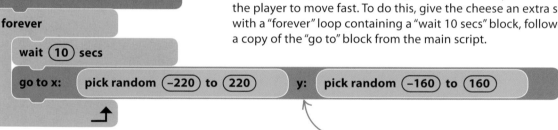

This block picks a random location for the cheese.

▷ **Don't touch the walls**

Make the game end if Mimi touches the walls of the maze. Add a script to the Maze sprite to send the message "GameOver" if she touches the maze. This makes the game much harder. To make it even harder, try switching the player's controls from the keyboard to the computer mouse. The game then becomes a test of a steady hand.

# Adding instructions

Players like to see a game's instructions clearly before they start playing. Here are three ways of including instructions.

▽ **Project page**

The easiest way to include instructions is to simply type them in the instructions box on the project page. You need to log in to an online Scratch account to do this.

Type the instructions here.

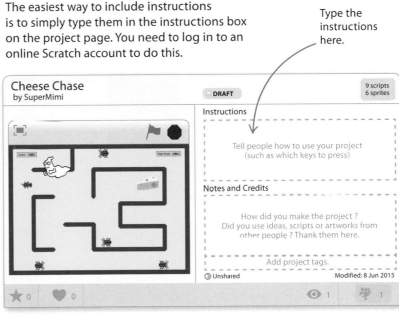

▽ **Instructions sprite**

You can use the paint editor to create an Instructions sprite in the same way that you created the Game Over sprite. Give it the following script to show the sprite at the start of the game and to hide it once the player presses the space bar.

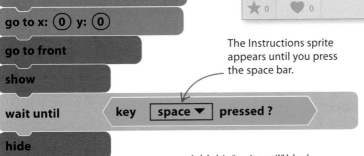

The Instructions sprite appears until you press the space bar.

Add this "wait until" block to the start of every other sprite's script so they don't start moving until the game begins.

▽ **Speech bubbles**

Make your game characters tell the player the instructions using speech bubbles. Add a "say" block to the start of Mimi's script to explain the game. Don't forget to add "wait" blocks to the enemies' scripts—otherwise there's a risk you'll lose before you start!

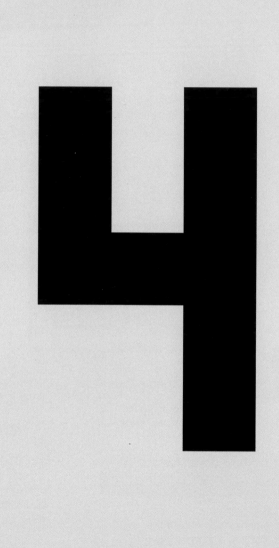

# Circle
# Wars

# How to build Circle Wars

**Lightning reactions are essential in Circle Wars, a fast-paced game in which you hunt green circles while being chased by red ones. The game uses Scratch's clones feature, which can turn a single sprite into an army of sinister copies.**

## AIM OF THE GAME

Move the blue circle around the screen using the mouse. Collect the pale green circles, but avoid the red ones that march toward you like a zombie army. The solid green and solid red circles drop clones of themselves as they roam around. Score more than 20 points to win and go below –20 to lose.

◁ **Player**
The player is the blue circle. If you don't keep moving quickly, the enemy circles will soon overwhelm you.

◁ **Friends**
The friendly circles are green. When you touch one, you score a point and the circle disappears with a pop.

◁ **Enemies**
Steer clear of the red enemy circles. Touch one and it takes three points off your score, before vanishing with a clash of cymbals.

The timer shows how long each game takes.

The score rises or falls as green and red clones are touched by the player.

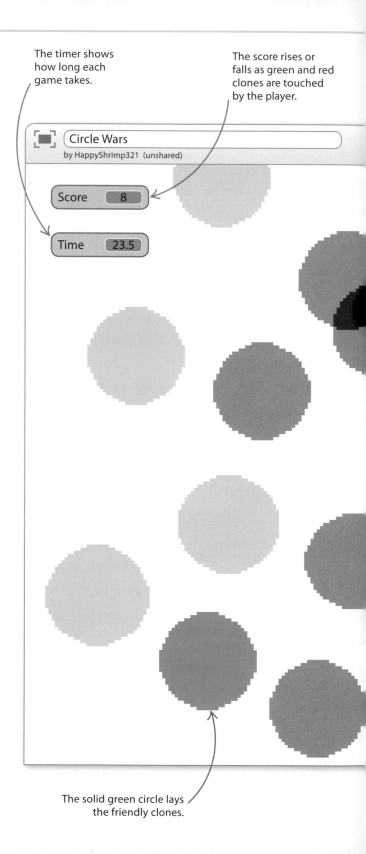

Circle Wars
by HappyShrimp321 (unshared)

Score    8

Time    23.5

The solid green circle lays the friendly clones.

The solid red circle lays the enemy clones.

Click the green flag to start a new game.

Click the stop sign to end a game.

**GAME CONTROLS**

Use a computer mouse or touchpad to control this game.

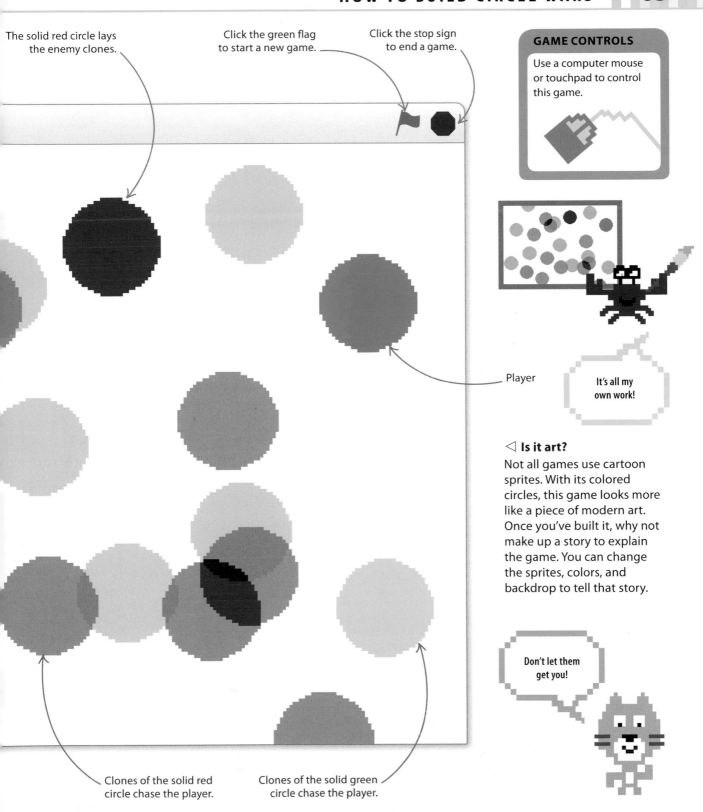

Player

It's all my own work!

◁ **Is it art?**
Not all games use cartoon sprites. With its colored circles, this game looks more like a piece of modern art. Once you've built it, why not make up a story to explain the game. You can change the sprites, colors, and backdrop to tell that story.

Don't let them get you!

Clones of the solid red circle chase the player.

Clones of the solid green circle chase the player.

# Creating the sprites

First you need to create the three sprites for the main game. These are all simple colored circles, so you can draw them yourself. Start by following these instructions to create the player's character—the blue circle.

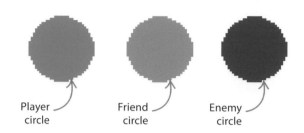

Player circle     Friend circle     Enemy circle

**1** Start a new project and name it "Circle Wars". Click the paintbrush symbol at the top of the sprites list to paint a new sprite.

New sprite:

Click here to paint a new sprite.

**2** To draw a blue circle, first select "Bitmap Mode" (bottom right). Then choose blue in the color palette.

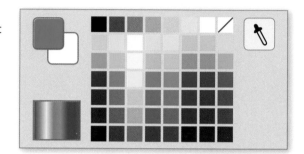

Circle tool

**3** Click the circle tool on the left and then select a solid color (rather than an outline) at the bottom left of the paint editor.

Select solid color.

**4** While holding down the shift key (this gives you a circle rather than an oval), click with the mouse and drag to draw a circle. The circle should be about the size of the cat's head. When you're happy with the circle's size, delete the cat sprite (right-click on it and select "delete").

Look on the stage to compare the size of your new sprite to the cat.

**5** You now need to center the sprite. Select the "Set costume center" tool (top right) and then click in the very center of the circle. Rename the sprite "Player" by clicking on the blue "i" in the sprites list.

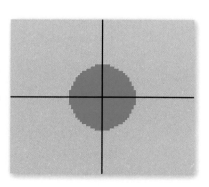

## Resizing the circle

If your circle is too big or too small, you can change the size of it by selecting either the "Grow" or "Shrink" tool on the bar along the top of the Scratch screen, then clicking on the circle.

Grow

Shrink

# Making friends and enemies

You can now make the green friend and red enemy circles. You can use other colors if you like, but make sure you can easily tell the three different circles apart.

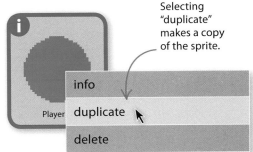

Selecting "duplicate" makes a copy of the sprite.

info
duplicate
delete

**6** Start by right-clicking on the Player sprite and selecting "duplicate". Do this twice. You'll now have three blue circles. Rename Player2 as "Friends" and Player3 as "Enemies".

**7** Select the Friends sprite and click the Costumes tab. Choose green in the color palette. Select the "Fill with color" tool and click inside the blue circle to make it turn green.

"Fill with color" tool

Click inside the blue circle to make it green.

**8** Repeat the steps for the Enemies sprite, but color this sprite red. You should now have three different colored sprites.

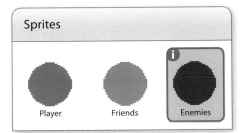

Sprites

Player      Friends      Enemies

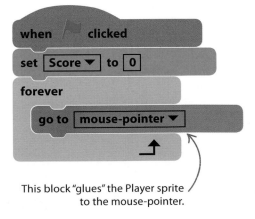

I have some friends and quite a few enemies!

---

# Instant player control

Now add a score display and a script to make the Player sprite stick to the mouse-pointer—just like in Star Hunter.

**9** Select the Player sprite, click Data, and make a variable called "Score" for all sprites. Then put a check in the variable's box to show "Score" on the stage.

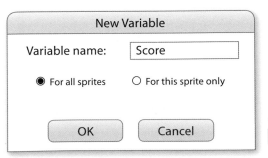

New Variable

Variable name:  Score

● For all sprites      ○ For this sprite only

OK          Cancel

Checking this box ensures that the score will appear on the stage.

☑ Score

**10** Add the script below to get the blue circle following the mouse. Read it through and make sure you understand what it does. Run the script to check it works. The red and green circles won't do anything yet.

```
when 🏴 clicked
set Score ▼ to 0
forever
    go to mouse-pointer ▼
```

This block "glues" the Player sprite to the mouse-pointer.

# March of the clones

From just two sprites—the green and red circles—you can create an army of friends and enemies to pursue the player's blue circle. You can do this through the magic of cloning. Before you create your clones, first get the Friends sprite moving randomly around the stage.

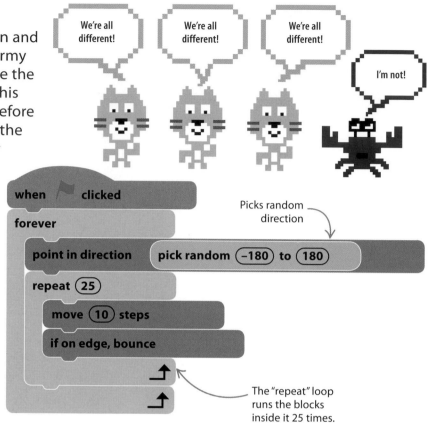

**11** Select the green Friends sprite. Add this script to make the circle bounce around the stage with a random change of direction every 250 steps.

```
when [flag] clicked
forever
    point in direction (pick random (-180) to (180))
    repeat (25)
        move (10) steps
        if on edge, bounce
```

Picks random direction

The "repeat" loop runs the blocks inside it 25 times.

**12** Run the project and watch the green circle's unpredictable journey. The Friends sprite moves 250 steps in 10-step jumps but it doesn't get stuck to the walls. After 250 steps, the "forever" loop goes back to the start. The sprite changes direction randomly and sets off again.

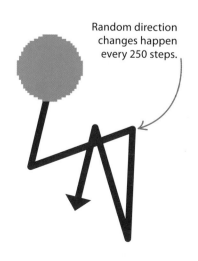

Random direction changes happen every 250 steps.

---

**··· EXPERT TIPS**

## Repeat loops

You've already seen "forever" loops that repeat a group of blocks nonstop. A "repeat" loop does a similar job, but it only repeats the blocks inside a fixed number of times. This type of loop is sometimes called a "for" loop, because it repeats *for* a certain number of times. The example shown here repeats an action four times to draw a square.

```
when [flag] clicked
pen down
repeat (4)
    move (100) steps
    turn (90) degrees
pen up
```

The blocks inside repeat 4 times.

After 4 repeats, the next block is run.

# Making clones

Now we're going to make our friendly clone army. These are the clones you need to catch to score points.

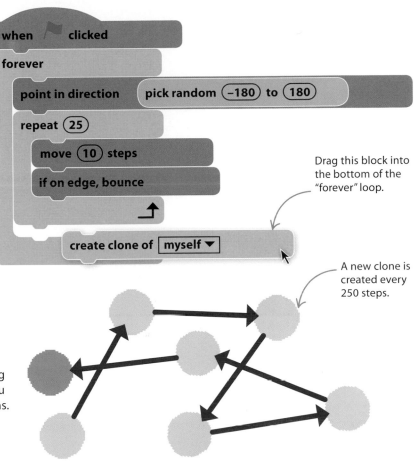

**13** Add a "create clone of myself" block as the last block in the "forever" loop. You'll find it in the yellow Control section. This block will create a clone of the Friends sprite after each 250-step movement.

Drag this block into the bottom of the "forever" loop.

A new clone is created every 250 steps.

**14** Run the project. At each change of direction, the sprite leaves a copy of itself—a clone. The clones aren't just pictures—they are fully working copies of the original sprite, and you can give them their own instructions.

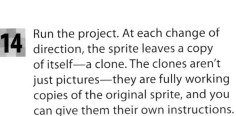

**15** New clones are controlled by a special script that starts with the block "when I start as a clone". Add the script below to the Friends sprite. The script tells each clone to move toward the Player sprite for 300 steps, after which the clone is deleted and vanishes from the stage. The clones move one step at a time. They move more slowly than the original Friends sprite, which moves in 10-step jumps.

All clones run their own copy of this script.

This block makes all the clones transparent.

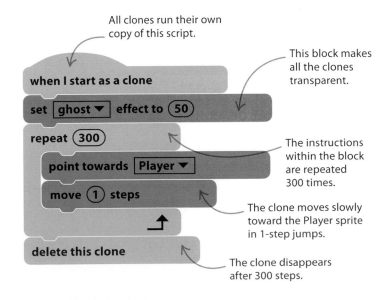

The instructions within the block are repeated 300 times.

The clone moves slowly toward the Player sprite in 1-step jumps.

**16** Run the script and watch the green clones advance slowly toward the Player sprite. Don't worry—they're the good guys!

The clone disappears after 300 steps.

# Destroying clones

The last part of the script for the Friends clone checks if the clone is touching the Player. If it is, the clone gets deleted.

**17** Add an "if then" block containing the blocks shown here to check whether the clone is touching the Player sprite after each move. Try running the project now—the score should increase as you touch green circles, which instantly disappear with a pop.

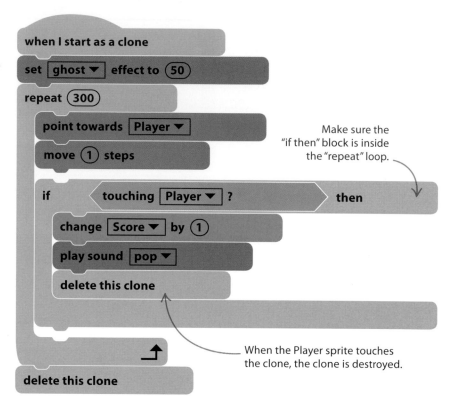

when I start as a clone
set ghost ▼ effect to 50
repeat 300
  point towards Player ▼
  move 1 steps
  if touching Player ▼ ? then
    change Score ▼ by 1
    play sound pop ▼
    delete this clone

delete this clone

Make sure the "if then" block is inside the "repeat" loop.

When the Player sprite touches the clone, the clone is destroyed.

= POP! =

**EXPERT TIPS**

# Clones

Clones are useful any time you want lots of copies of a sprite. Many programming languages let you make copies of things, but they are often called objects rather than clones.

Such languages are called "object oriented" languages and include Java and C++. In Scratch, there are three orange blocks that control clones, all found in the Control section.

create clone of myself ▼

△ This block creates a clone of the sprite. The clone is identical to the sprite and appears in the same position and facing the same direction, so you won't be able to see it until it moves.

when I start as a clone

△ When a clone starts, it runs the script headed with this block. Clones don't run the sprite's main script, but they can run all other scripts in the sprite's scripts area, such as scripts triggered by messages.

delete this clone

△ This block gets rid of the clone. All clones disappear from the stage when a project stops, leaving just the original sprite.

# Enemy clones

Now you need to add scripts to the Enemies sprite to make it produce clones that chase the Player. You can do this by copying the scripts from the Friends sprite across to the Enemies sprite.

**18** To copy scripts, just click, drag, and drop scripts from one sprite onto another. Drag the two scripts you made for the Friends sprite onto the Enemies sprite, one at a time. This makes copies of the scripts in the Enemies sprite.

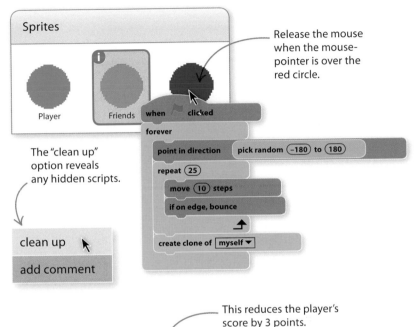

Release the mouse when the mouse-pointer is over the red circle.

The "clean up" option reveals any hidden scripts.

```
when [flag] clicked
forever
    point in direction (pick random (-180) to (180))
    repeat (25)
        move (10) steps
        if on edge, bounce
    create clone of [myself ▼]
```

clean up

add comment

**19** Select the Enemies sprite. The scripts you dragged and dropped will probably be on top of one another, because any copied script just appears at the top left of the scripts area. To rearrange them, right-click on the background and select "clean up".

**20** Now adjust the Enemies clone script so that it takes points away when the Player touches a red clone. Alter the "change Score by" block so it changes the score by −3 instead of +1. You really want to avoid those nasty red enemies!

This reduces the player's score by 3 points.

```
change [Score ▼] by (-3)
```

**21** Add a sound to tell the player that points have been lost. Load the cymbal sound into the Enemies sprite by selecting "cymbal" in the sound library. Alter the script to play "cymbal", not "pop". You'll now hear which type of clone you've touched.

Change the script to play a cymbal sound.

```
play sound [cymbal ▼]
```

**22** Run the project. Check that you now have both red and green clones, and that touching a red clone takes 3 points off your score.

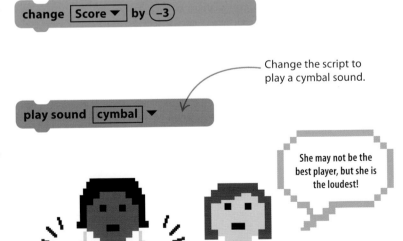

She may not be the best player, but she is the loudest!

# Win or lose?

You've created two ever-expanding clone armies: one of friendly circles that help you win points, and one of evil circles that make you lose points. Next you need to add the code that tells you if you've won or lost the game.

**23** Add the new "if then" blocks shown here to the Player sprite. They check your score. If the score is greater than 20, you win, and a thought bubble with the word "Victory!" appears. If the score is less than –20, you lose, and the sprite thinks "Defeat!"

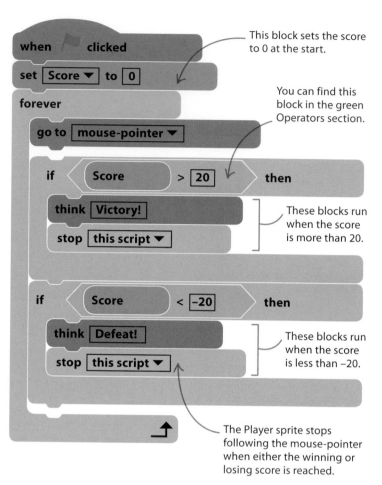

This block sets the score to 0 at the start.

You can find this block in the green Operators section.

These blocks run when the score is more than 20.

These blocks run when the score is less than –20.

The Player sprite stops following the mouse-pointer when either the winning or losing score is reached.

---

## LINGO

# Comparison operators

Earlier we saw how you can use "if then" blocks to create true or false statements—also known as Boolean expressions—that lead to different outcomes. For example, in Star Hunter, "if touching cat then play sound fairydust" makes a sound play only when the cat gets a star. We can do the same thing with numbers by using what are called comparison operators:

2 < 5   is less than

3 = 3   equals

5 > 1   is more than

When we add these to "if then" blocks, they create statements that are either true or false. In Circle Wars, the "is more than" operator tells you that you've won the game when you score over 20.

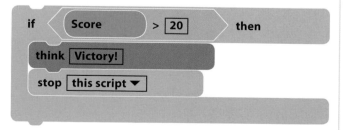

**24** Run the game. Try to touch only the green circles. Check that the game ends when the key scores are reached, and check that the Player sprite thinks "Victory!" or "Defeat!" You can reduce the score needed to win if you find it too difficult. But don't make the game too easy—Circle Wars is meant to be a challenge!

I am the champion!

## Adding a timer

To add some competition to the game, you can include an on-screen timer that shows players how long they take to complete a game.

**25** Click on the Data section and make a variable "Time" for all sprites. To show it on the stage, check the box next to the variable's block. Select the Player sprite. Click on Sensing in the blocks palette. Add "reset timer" to the Player's script, just before the "forever" loop. Go back to Data and drag a "set Time to" block to the script and add "timer" to it, making it the last instruction in the forever loop.

**26** By copying "timer" to the variable "Time", each trip around the loop will now display the time on the stage. But the moment the player wins or loses, the time stops being updated (the script is stopped) and the total time it took to win or lose is shown.

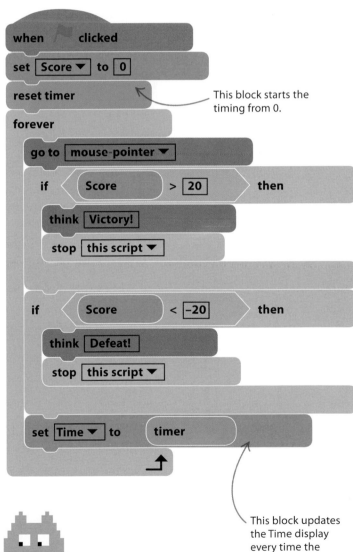

This block starts the timing from 0.

This block updates the Time display every time the loop repeats.

Time 41.573

Total number of seconds in the game

I think it must be lunch time!

# Instructions

Players need to know the rules of the game. Create a special sprite that shows the instructions for Circle Wars when the game begins.

Use black for the text.

Choosing a light background color will make the text easier to read.

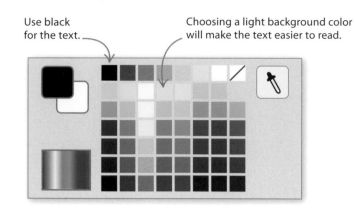

**27** Use the paintbrush symbol to create a new sprite and rename it "Instructions". Select "Bitmap Mode" and choose a color. Select the "Fill with color" tool and click on the drawing area to fill it with your chosen color.

"Fill with color" tool

**28** Now select black from the palette as the color for the text. Then choose the text tool and type out the instructions shown here.

Text tool

**29** If the text doesn't fit, use the select tool to resize it by pulling the corner points in or out. When you've finished, click outside the box around the text to stop editing.

"Select" tool

You may want to decorate your instructions with colored circles.

You are the blue circle.
Move using the mouse.
Be quick!

Try to touch the friendly green circles.
Each one gives you 1 point.
Avoid the enemy red circles.
Each one you touch takes 3 points.

Score more than 20 to win.
Score less than –20 and you lose.

Press the space bar to start!

 **GAME DESIGN**

## Game stories

Computer games usually have a story to explain why the action in the game is happening. At the moment, Circle Wars has no story. Can you make one up? It could be a battle in space, with a blue spaceship saving friendly green spaceships and trying to avoid being hit by the red enemy craft. Let your imagination run riot! Including some of the story in your instructions will help make the game more interesting and exciting for the player.

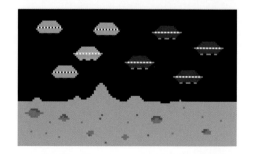

**30** Add this script to the sprite to show the instructions on the stage at the start of the game. Read it carefully. Can you see how it works?

These blocks show the instructions in the center of the screen in front of other sprites.

This block hides the Instruction sprite when the player presses the space bar to start playing.

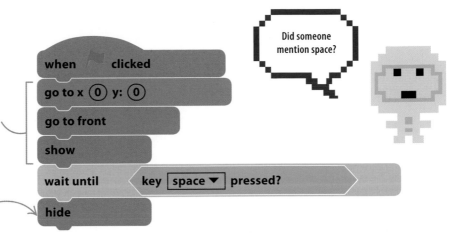

Did someone mention space?

```
when [flag] clicked
go to x (0) y: (0)
go to front
show
wait until < key [space ▼] pressed? >
hide
```

**31** You also need to add a "wait until key space pressed" block immediately after the green flag blocks in the Player, Friends, and Enemies sprites' scripts. This will hold back all the action until the space bar is pressed.

**32** Run the project and your instructions should appear, filling the screen until you press the space bar. Players will have plenty of time to read and understand the instructions, letting them start the game when they're ready.

Add a "wait until key space pressed" block to the scripts of all three sprites.

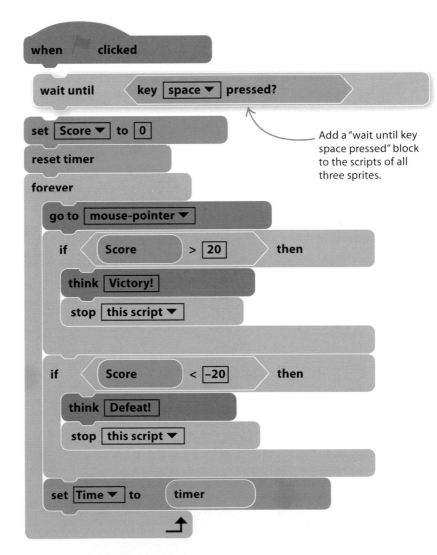

```
when [flag] clicked
wait until < key [space ▼] pressed? >
set [Score ▼] to [0]
reset timer
forever
    go to [mouse-pointer ▼]
    if < Score > [20] > then
        think [Victory!]
        stop [this script ▼]
    if < Score < [-20] > then
        think [Defeat!]
        stop [this script ▼]
    set [Time ▼] to (timer)
```

I'm ready to play!

# Hacks and tweaks

You've got Circle Wars working—well done!
Now to personalize it and make it your own.
Try these suggestions and your own ideas.
Once you've created something unique, why
not share it on the Scratch projects website?

△ **Find a balance**
Experiment with different speeds, or change
how many points you win or lose for touching
Friends and Enemies. It's not difficult to make
the game very hard or very easy, but can you
find a balance to make it just the right level?

▽ **What's the story?**
Did you think of a story to explain what's going on in
Circle Wars? Maybe it's the attack of the dragons, and
the princess player has to eat cakes to survive? Add
some scenery and music to the game to fit with that
story. Experiment with different stories and looks.

▷ **The war's over!**
Add a broadcast message to
reveal a "Game over!" sprite when
the player wins or loses, like you
did in Cheese Chase. You can
change the text of the "Game
over!" sprite so that it relates to
your story about the game.

▷ **Slow down, blue!**
To make things tricky, change
the blue circle's script so that it
no longer "sticks" to the mouse
pointer but chases slowly after
it. You could also invent simple
keyboard controls for the sprite.

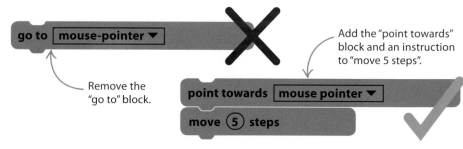

Remove the
"go to" block.

Add the "point towards"
block and an instruction
to "move 5 steps".

▽ **Tweak the timer**
The number in the timer flickers because it shows lots of
decimal places. To round the value so it shows only whole
seconds, use the green "round" block near the bottom of
the Operators section. Try adding a "Best time" for winning
players, just as you added a "High score" in Cheese Chase.

That's their best
time yet!

## ▽ Change the colors

Vary the clones' colors. Click on the Friends sprite. Add the "set color effect to" block from the Looks section to the sprite's clone script. Then drag "pick random" from Operators into the block's window and change the values to –30 and 30. Do the same for the Enemies sprite. New clones will now have different colors!

Green and blue circles are friends.

Orange, yellow, pink, and purple circles are enemies.

```
when I start as a clone
set  color ▼  effect to    pick random (–30) to (30)
set  ghost ▼  effect to (50)
repeat (300)
```

Insert this instruction immediately after "when I start as a clone".

## ▷ Change the size

Add the "change size by" block to the scripts of both the Friends and Enemies sprites to make each clone a random size. Alter the scoring so that the size of the circle you touch determines how many points you score. You'll also need to change the totals needed to win or lose. Try more than 2,000 points for victory, and less than –2,000 for defeat.

From green Operators section

```
when I start as a clone
change size by       pick random (–30) to (30)
set  ghost ▼  effect to (50)
repeat (300)
```

Change the values to "–30" and "30".

Change the Friends' score value to this.

```
change  Score ▼  by    size
```

```
change  Score ▼  by   (0) – size
```

Use this scoring for Enemies.

The bigger the clone, the more points you win or lose.

## ◁ Shape shifting

Introduce another shape into the game. It could be a square that eats red circles, a triangle that runs away from the player, a hexagon that makes the player shrink or grow, or anything else you want to try.

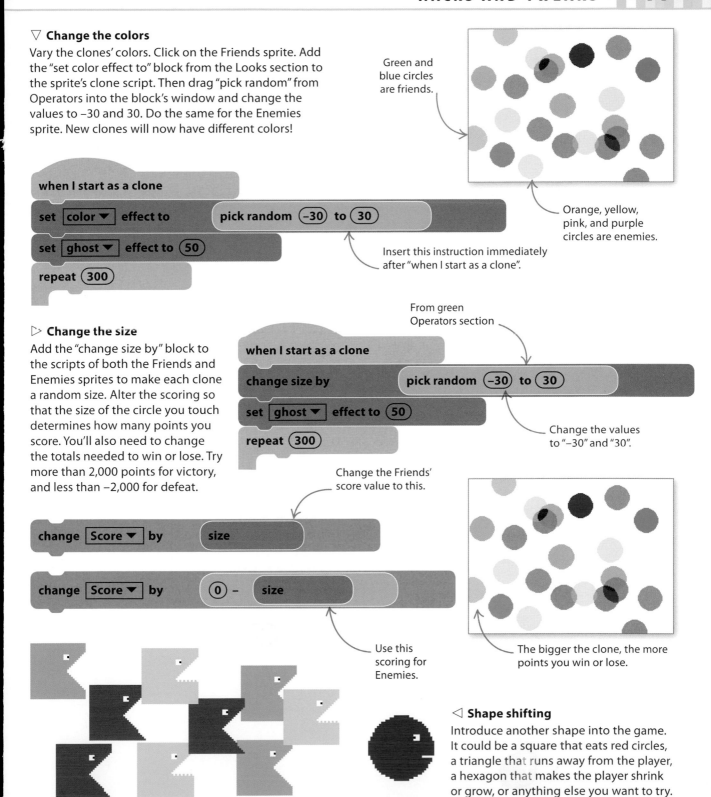

# Jumpy Monkey

# How to build Jumpy Monkey

In the real world there are laws you just can't break. For example, the law of gravity means that something that goes up must always come down again. Jumpy Monkey shows you how to add gravity to your game worlds.

## AIM OF THE GAME

The monkey is on a mission to collect bananas. Choose which direction he leaps in and how fast he goes. You need to send him over the palm tree to grab the bananas using the fewest possible jumps.

◁ **Launcher**
Point this arrow in the direction you want to launch the monkey by using the left and right arrow keys.

◁ **Monkey**
Select the monkey's launch speed with the up and down arrow keys, then press the space key to launch him.

◁ **Bananas**
If the monkey touches any of the bananas he will eat them. Keep going until he eats all the bananas.

The instructions appear on the game at the start.

Jumpy Monkey
by FunkyMonkey66 (unshared)

SET LAUNCH ANGLE ←→
SET LAUNCH SPEED ↑↓
PRESS SPACE TO FIRE

LaunchSpeed 11

The monkey is launched from the arrow when you press the space key.

This number shows you how fast the monkey will fly once he is launched.

The monkey flies through the air like a cannonball.

**GAME CONTROLS**

Players use the arrow keys and space key on the keyboard as game controls.

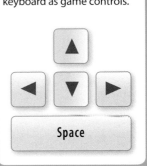

Space

◁ **Flying monkey**
Try to collect all the bananas using as few launches as possible. The game will record how many launches you use.

There are three bunches of bananas to collect each time you play the game.

Avoid the tree—the monkey can't fly through it.

**Down with gravity!**

# Launching the monkey

This game uses a big arrow to help the player choose the monkey's precise launch direction. We'll ignore gravity to start off with, but you'll need to add it later to get the monkey past the tree.

**1** Start a new project and call it "Jumpy Monkey". Delete the cat sprite and load two sprites from the library—"Monkey2" and "Arrow1". Select the arrow sprite and rename it "Launcher" by clicking on the "i" and typing the new name into the box.

**2** Go to Data, select "make a variable", and add a variable called "LaunchSpeed". The new variable will automatically show up on the stage.

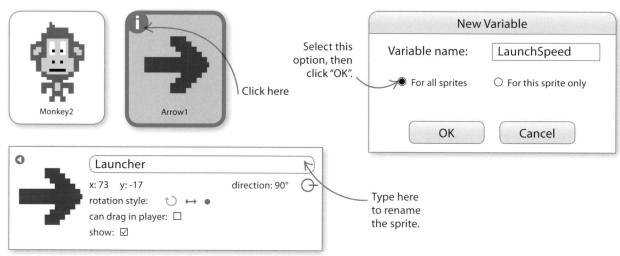

Click here

Select this option, then click "OK".

New Variable

Variable name:    LaunchSpeed

● For all sprites    ○ For this sprite only

OK      Cancel

Launcher

x: 73   y: -17        direction: 90°

rotation style: ↻ ↔ •

can drag in player: ☐

show: ☑

Type here to rename the sprite.

**3** Select the Launcher sprite, then add these three scripts to set up the Launcher and allow the player to control its angle using the left and right arrow keys on the keyboard. The direction of the arrow is the direction that the monkey will launch. Run the scripts and try turning the arrow.

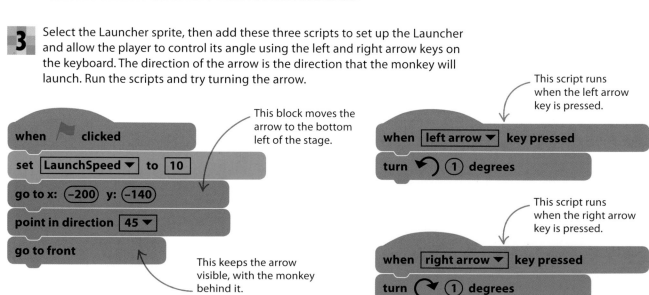

This block moves the arrow to the bottom left of the stage.

This keeps the arrow visible, with the monkey behind it.

This script runs when the left arrow key is pressed.

This script runs when the right arrow key is pressed.

```
when [flag] clicked
set LaunchSpeed ▼ to 10
go to x: (-200) y: (-140)
point in direction 45 ▼
go to front
```

```
when left arrow ▼ key pressed
turn ↺ (1) degrees
```

```
when right arrow ▼ key pressed
turn ↻ (1) degrees
```

**4** Now that you can aim, you need controls to set the speed of the launch. Add these scripts to change the speed using the up and down arrow keys.

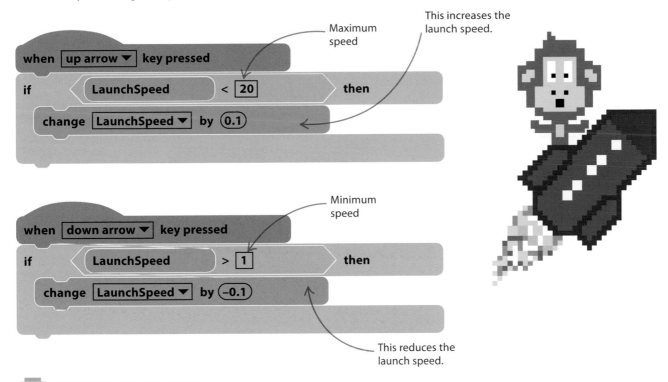

Maximum speed

This increases the launch speed.

```
when up arrow ▼ key pressed
if    < LaunchSpeed < 20 > then
    change LaunchSpeed ▼ by (0.1)
```

Minimum speed

```
when down arrow ▼ key pressed
if    < LaunchSpeed > 1 > then
    change LaunchSpeed ▼ by (-0.1)
```

This reduces the launch speed.

. . . LINGO

## Events

The key presses and mouse clicks that a computer detects are known as events. The brown Events blocks in Scratch trigger a script whenever a particular event occurs. We've seen them used with messages in Cheese Chase, but Scratch also lets you trigger scripts using keys, mouse clicks, sound levels, and even movement detected by a webcam. Don't be afraid to experiment.

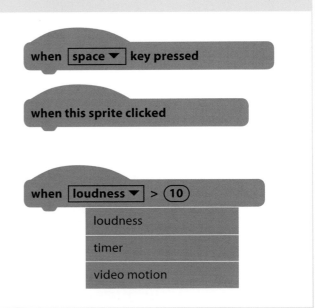

```
when space ▼ key pressed
```

```
when this sprite clicked
```

```
when loudness ▼ > (10)
```

| loudness |
| timer |
| video motion |

▷ **Setting things off**
Events blocks such as these are used to trigger a script whenever the event they describe occurs.

**5** Now select the Monkey sprite. Add this script to shrink him down to the right size and move him behind the Launcher.

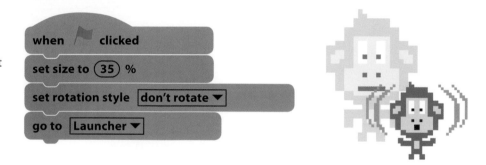

when 🏳 clicked

set size to (35) %

set rotation style | don't rotate ▼ |

go to | Launcher ▼ |

**6** To launch the monkey when the space bar is pressed, add this new script to the Monkey sprite. "Repeat until" is a new type of loop block that keeps repeating the block inside until the condition becomes true—in this case, the monkey keeps moving until it touches the edge of the stage.

This makes the monkey's direction match the direction of the launch arrow.

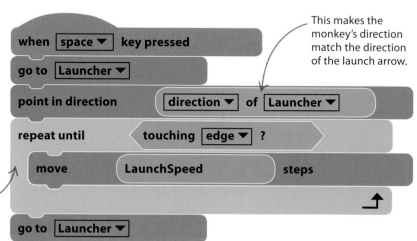

when | space ▼ | key pressed

go to | Launcher ▼ |

point in direction ( | direction ▼ | of | Launcher ▼ | )

repeat until ⟨ touching | edge ▼ | ? ⟩

     move ( LaunchSpeed ) steps

go to | Launcher ▼ |

The "repeat until" block keeps the monkey moving to the edge of the stage.

---

**⸬ EXPERT TIPS**

## "repeat until"

Do you want to keep repeating an action only until something happens and then move on to the rest of the script? The "repeat until" block can help your code when "forever" and "repeat" loops aren't flexible enough. Most programming languages use similar loops, but some call them "while" loops—these continue *while* the condition is true, rather than looping *until* the condition is true. There are always different ways to think about the same problem.

**7** Try setting the Launcher angle and speed using the arrow keys, and pressing the space bar to fire the monkey. He goes in a completely straight line until he hits the edge of the stage. Real things don't do this—they fall back toward the ground as they move. We'll add gravity to the game later to make the monkey behave realistically.

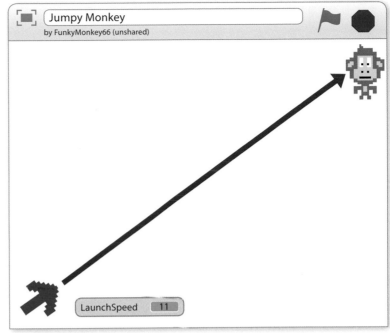

```
[■]  Jumpy Monkey
     by FunkyMonkey66 (unshared)

                    LaunchSpeed   11
```

## Bananas and palm trees

The point of this game is for the monkey to collect bananas. By using clones, you can add just one Bananas sprite but give the monkey plenty of fruit to aim for.

**8** Add the Bananas sprite to the project. Make a variable for all sprites called "NumBananas" to keep track of the number of bananas on the stage—start with three. Build the following script to clone the bananas, but don't run it yet because you still need to tell the clones what to do.

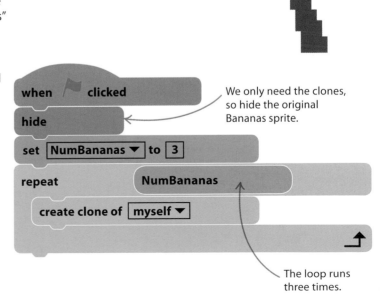

```
when  ⚑  clicked
hide
set  NumBananas ▼  to  3
repeat              NumBananas
    create clone of  myself ▼
                                    ↰
```

We only need the clones, so hide the original Bananas sprite.

The loop runs three times.

**9**   Add the next script to place each banana clone in a random spot on the right of the stage, change how it looks, and make sure it's not hidden. The clone will wait for the monkey to touch it and then disappear. If it's the last banana, it sends a "GameOver" message, which you need to create as a new message.

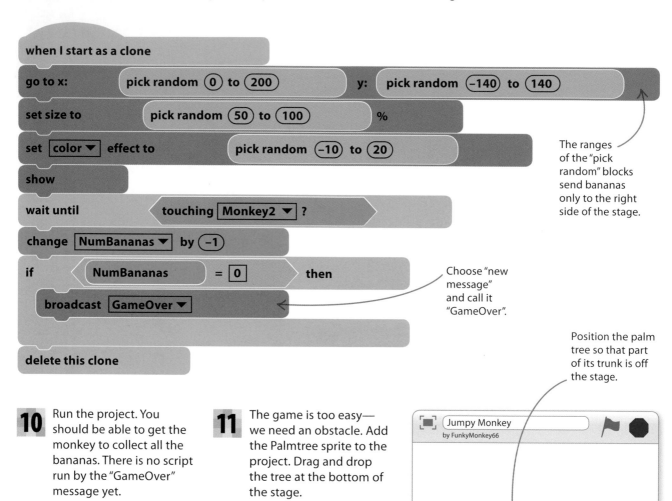

The ranges of the "pick random" blocks send bananas only to the right side of the stage.

Choose "new message" and call it "GameOver".

```
when I start as a clone
go to x: pick random (0) to (200)   y:  pick random (-140) to (140)
set size to   pick random (50) to (100)   %
set [color ▼] effect to   pick random (-10) to (20)
show
wait until   touching [Monkey2 ▼] ?
change [NumBananas ▼] by (-1)
if   NumBananas = 0   then
    broadcast [GameOver ▼]

delete this clone
```

Position the palm tree so that part of its trunk is off the stage.

**10**  Run the project. You should be able to get the monkey to collect all the bananas. There is no script run by the "GameOver" message yet.

**11**  The game is too easy—we need an obstacle. Add the Palmtree sprite to the project. Drag and drop the tree at the bottom of the stage.

Jumpy Monkey
by FunkyMonkey66

Yum yum!

△ **Tree on stage**

Make sure your palm tree is slightly off-center, toward the left of the stage, or the bananas will get stuck behind the tree and the game won't work.

**12** At the moment, the monkey can fly straight through the tree. Change his script so that he stops flying if he touches it.

The current script

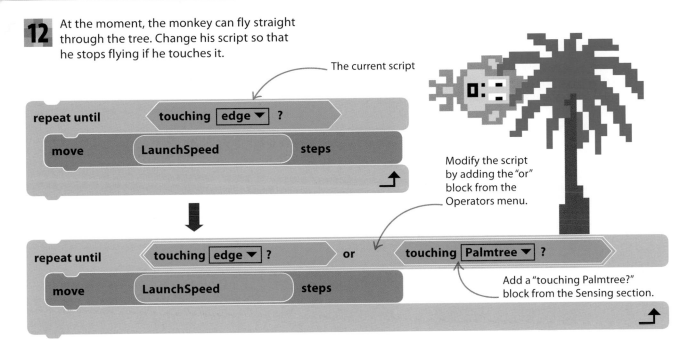

repeat until  [ touching [edge ▼] ? ]
  move  [LaunchSpeed] steps
  ↰

⬇

repeat until  [ touching [edge ▼] ? ] ⟩ **or** ⟨ touching [Palmtree ▼] ? ]
  move  [LaunchSpeed] steps
  ↰

Modify the script by adding the "or" block from the Operators menu.

Add a "touching Palmtree?" block from the Sensing section.

**13** Run the project. The monkey should stop flying when he hits the tree, which makes any bananas to the right of the tree impossible to reach. Don't worry, gravity will come to the rescue soon.

I want those bananas!

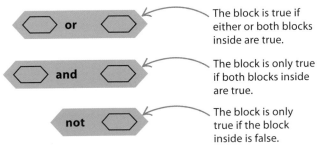

**14** Make two more variables for all sprites: "FallSpeed" and "Gravity". Then add a "set Gravity" block to the monkey's "when clicked" script and amend his "when space key pressed" script as shown below. The new blocks use variables to simulate gravity. "FallSpeed" keeps track of how many steps the monkey needs to be moved down by gravity. The value of "Gravity" is how much "FallSpeed" increases each time the monkey moves.

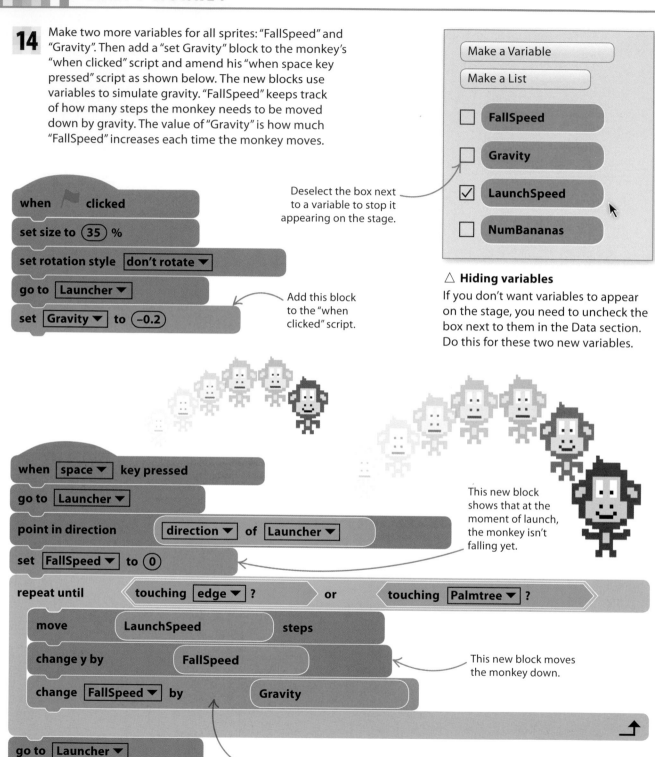

Deselect the box next to a variable to stop it appearing on the stage.

△ **Hiding variables**
If you don't want variables to appear on the stage, you need to uncheck the box next to them in the Data section. Do this for these two new variables.

Add this block to the "when clicked" script.

This new block shows that at the moment of launch, the monkey isn't falling yet.

This new block moves the monkey down.

This new block contains the variable "Gravity", which makes the monkey fall faster each time the loop runs.

# Real world gravity

In the real world, when you try to throw something in a straight line it curves slowly back toward the ground as gravity pulls it down. To make the game work in the same way, you move the monkey along the straight line, but also add a downward move after each shift along that line, to create the same effect as the constant downward tug of gravity. This allows the monkey's movement to seem natural, making the game more engaging.

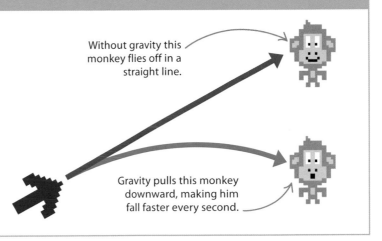

Without gravity this monkey flies off in a straight line.

Gravity pulls this monkey downward, making him fall faster every second.

**15** Run the project again—you can now direct the monkey over the tree to reach the tricky low bananas. But how exactly is the Scratch gravity working? Every second, the monkey falls a little bit faster than the second before, creating a downward curve.

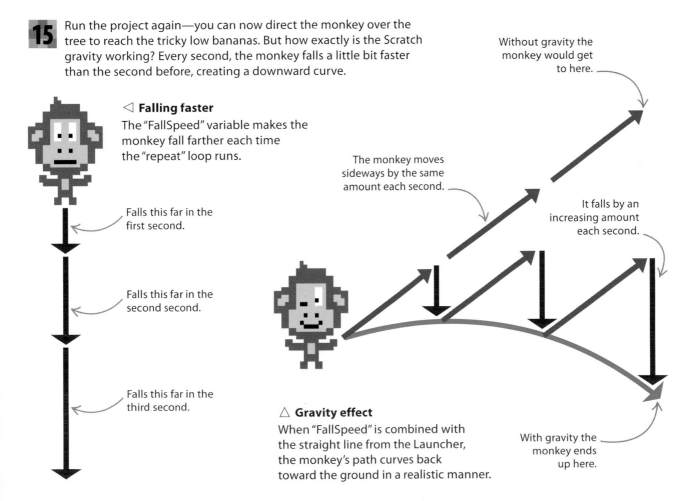

◁ **Falling faster**
The "FallSpeed" variable makes the monkey fall farther each time the "repeat" loop runs.

Falls this far in the first second.

Falls this far in the second second.

Falls this far in the third second.

Without gravity the monkey would get to here.

The monkey moves sideways by the same amount each second.

It falls by an increasing amount each second.

△ **Gravity effect**
When "FallSpeed" is combined with the straight line from the Launcher, the monkey's path curves back toward the ground in a realistic manner.

With gravity the monkey ends up here.

## Game over

When the monkey has collected all the bananas, a "GameOver" message is broadcast, ending the game. Make a sign to go with it to tell the player how many launches were used to collect the bananas.

**16** Click the paintbrush symbol to paint a new sprite and make a sign like the one below, leaving a gap in the text where the number of launches will go. You can make the sign as plain or as decorative as you like. Name the new sprite "GameOver".

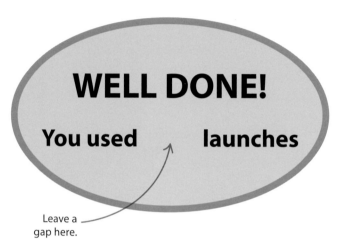

Leave a gap here.

**17** Now add a variable for all sprites to count the number of launches. Call this variable "Launches", show it on the stage, and right-click on it to change it to "large readout". This shows just the value and not the name of the variable. You'll reposition the launch counter later.

Right-click on "Launches" on the stage.

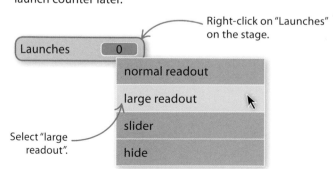

Select "large readout".

**18** Now add these scripts to your sign. Together, they will count the number of times you launch the monkey and will display that number at the end of the game.

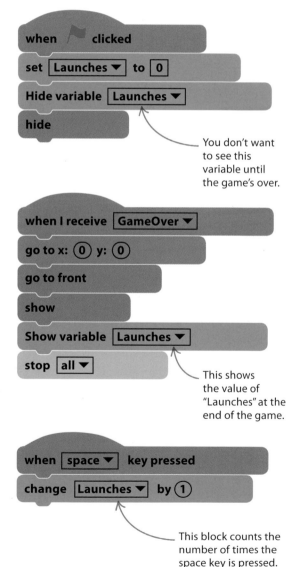

You don't want to see this variable until the game's over.

This shows the value of "Launches" at the end of the game.

This block counts the number of times the space key is pressed.

**19** Run the game and collect all the bananas. When you see the "Game Over" sign on the stage, drag the "Launches" counter into the gap in the sign. Scratch will remember its position in future games, so the sign will always be in the right place.

Drag the "Launches" number into the gap you left in the sign.

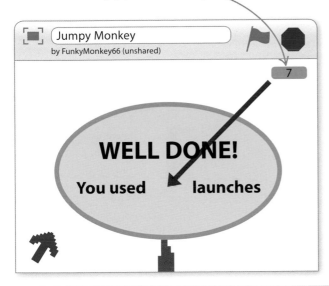

**20** To add a backdrop, click on the stage information area in the bottom left and then choose the Backdrop tab at the top. Either paint your own scenery or load an image from the library. Use the text tool to add the game's instructions to the image, as shown below.

Draw the arrows with the pencil or paintbrush tool.

## Make some noise

To make the game more interesting, you can add some sound effects. Follow the instructions below to play different sounds when the monkey is launched and when he eats the bananas.

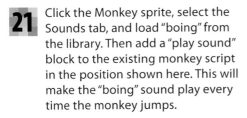

**21** Click the Monkey sprite, select the Sounds tab, and load "boing" from the library. Then add a "play sound" block to the existing monkey script in the position shown here. This will make the "boing" sound play every time the monkey jumps.

**22** Click the Bananas sprite and load "chomp" from the sound library. Then add a "play sound" block to the existing banana script in the position shown here. Now the "chomping" sound will play each time the monkey gets a banana.

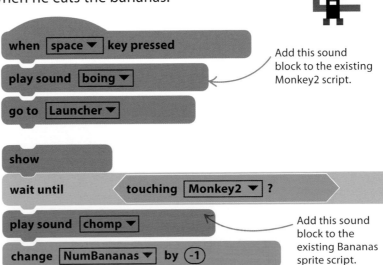

Add this sound block to the existing Monkey2 script.

Add this sound block to the existing Bananas sprite script.

# Playing with gravity

Add a slider to the game to allow you to experiment with the "Gravity" variable. The slider will allow you to tweak the "Gravity" value—you can even make the monkey fall upward.

**23** To adjust gravity in your game world, show the "Gravity" variable on the stage by checking its box in the Data section. Then right-click the variable display on the stage and select "slider". The slider lets you change the value of a variable on the stage.

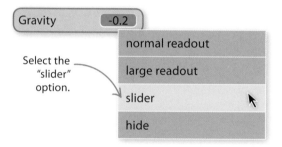

Select the "slider" option.

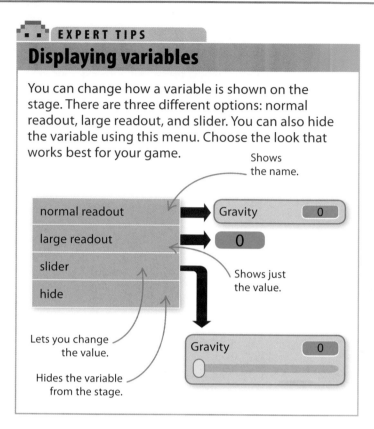

EXPERT TIPS

## Displaying variables

You can change how a variable is shown on the stage. There are three different options: normal readout, large readout, and slider. You can also hide the variable using this menu. Choose the look that works best for your game.

Shows the name.

Shows just the value.

Lets you change the value.

Hides the variable from the stage.

**24** To set the range of the variable, right-click on the slider and type in the minimum and maximum values—for this game use −2.0 and 2.0. Make sure you type 2.0 not just 2, or the slider will only allow you to select whole numbers within the range.

Set the range of the slider by right-clicking on the slider again.

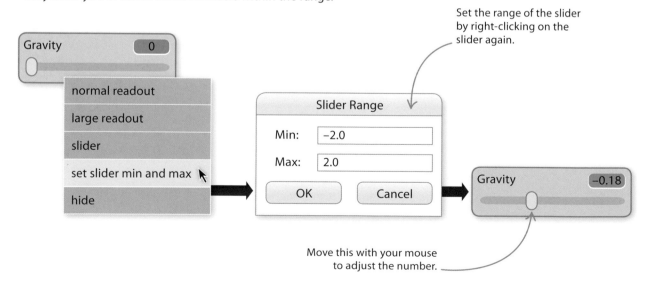

Move this with your mouse to adjust the number.

**25** Now play around with the gravity settings in this game using the slider. Using the suggested value of –0.2 works well, but take a look at what happens when you increase or decrease this number—if it is positive, the monkey will fall upward.

**26** When you've finished experimenting with gravity, right-click on the slider and select "hide" to return the game to normal. Now you know how gravity works, you could try making a version of the game with reverse gravity so the monkey falls upward. Think about what changes you'd need to make to the game for this to work, like moving the Launcher to fire downward.

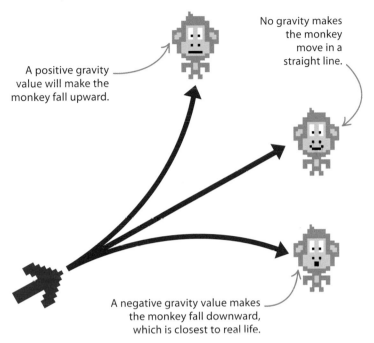

No gravity makes the monkey move in a straight line.

A positive gravity value will make the monkey fall upward.

A negative gravity value makes the monkey fall downward, which is closest to real life.

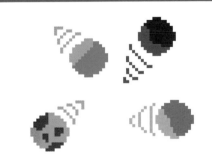

Help!!!

**GAME DESIGN**

## Game physics

Physics is the science of forces and movement in the real world. Game physics is all about getting that science into games, so that things react and move around in realistic ways—being pulled down by gravity, for instance, or bouncing. Programmers have to solve all types of physics problems to make games more realistic or fun. When objects collide, should they bounce or crunch? How should objects move when they go underwater or into space?

△ **Defying gravity**
Game physics doesn't have to be like real-world physics—you can create worlds with gravity that makes things fall upward or even sideways. Gravity can be much stronger or weaker than in real life—perhaps balls fly higher with each bounce, until they shoot off into space.

# Hacks and tweaks

Congratulations—you've built your first game with gravity. Once you've tried the game a few times, you can start to play around with the code to make the game your own. Here are a few ideas to try out.

◁ **Banana bonanza**
Try adding more bananas, making then bigger or smaller, and put them in different places on the screen.

▽ **Fruit salad**
Add more fruits with a different score for each type. You'll need to make a "Score" variable and add extra sprites—there are oranges and watermelons in the Scratch sprite library.

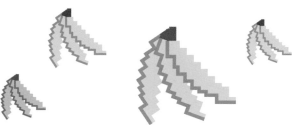

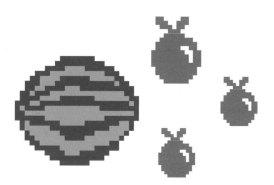

▽ **Beat the clock**
You can add a timer to make the player complete the game in a set time. Create a new variable called "TimeLeft" and add the script below to the Monkey2 sprite. Then create a new sprite, click on the Costumes tab, and make a sign that says "Time's Up!" Finally, add the two scripts on the right to this sprite.

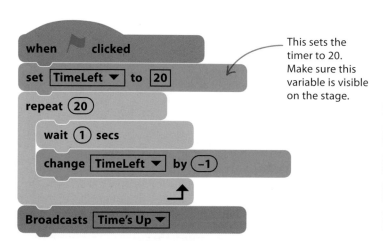

This sets the timer to 20. Make sure this variable is visible on the stage.

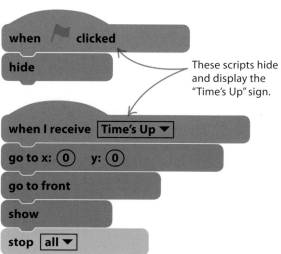

These scripts hide and display the "Time's Up" sign.

## ▽ Mouse control

You could use a computer mouse as the controller for this game instead of the keyboard. The three blocks below allow you to set the launch angle and speed as well as making the monkey jump. See if you can figure out some code to use them.

Use this block to make the monkey jump.

`mouse down?`

`distance to  mouse-pointer ▼`

This block could be used to set launch speed.

`point towards  mouse-pointer ▼`

Use this block to set launch angle.

## ▷ Bouncing bananas

To make the game a bit harder, you could try changing the Bananas sprite scripts so that the bananas bounce up and down on the stage.

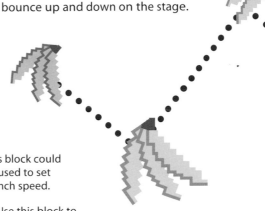

## ▷ Danger! Snake!

Add another challenge by creating an obstacle that gets in the monkey's way or maybe ends the game—perhaps a giant monkey-eating snake or spider?

## ▽ Bug or bonus?

You might have discovered that you can adjust the monkey's speed in flight with the arrow keys. You can fix this by adding a new variable, "MonkeySpeed", and copying the value of "LaunchSpeed" into it at launch. Then use MonkeySpeed not LaunchSpeed in the move block for the monkey. Or, if you enjoy being able to change the monkey's speed, leave the game as it is.

## ▽ Launch speed slide

You've already tried adding a slider to control gravity. You could also add a slider to adjust launch speed.

Sliders let you change these variables using the mouse instead of the arrow keys.

# Index

Page numbers in **bold** refer to main entries.

# Acknowledgments

Dorling Kindersley would like to thank: Bahja Norwood for editorial assistance and testing; Caroline Hunt for proofreading; and Helen Peters for the index.

Dorling Kindersley India would like to thank Riji Raju for editorial assistance.

Scratch is developed by the Lifelong Kindergarten Group at MIT Media Lab. See **http://scratch.mit.edu**